THE KINGFISHER
ATLAS OF THE
ANCIENT
WORLD

Simon Adams

Illustrated by Katherine Baxter

KINGFISHER

KINGFISHER

Kingfisher Publications Plc
New Penderel House
283–288 High Holborn
London WC1V 7HZ
www.kingfisherpub.com

Senior editor: Catherine Brereton
Senior designers: Carol Ann Davis, Malcolm Parchment
Assistant designer: Jack Clucas
Cover designer: Mike Buckley
Consultant: Dr Miles Russell, Bournemouth University
Picture research manager: Cee Weston-Baker
Senior production controller: Lindsey Scott
DTP co-ordinator: Catherine Hibbert
Proof-reader: Sheila Clewley

Cartography by: Anderson Geographics Limited, Warfield, Berkshire

First published by Kingfisher Publications Plc 2006
10 9 8 7 6 5 4 3 2 1

1TR/0406/SHENS/CLSN(CLSN)/128MA/C

ISBN-13: 978 0 7534 1174 2
ISBN-10: 0 7534 1174 1

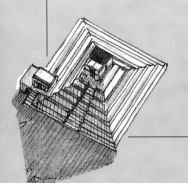

CONTENTS

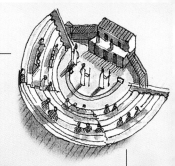

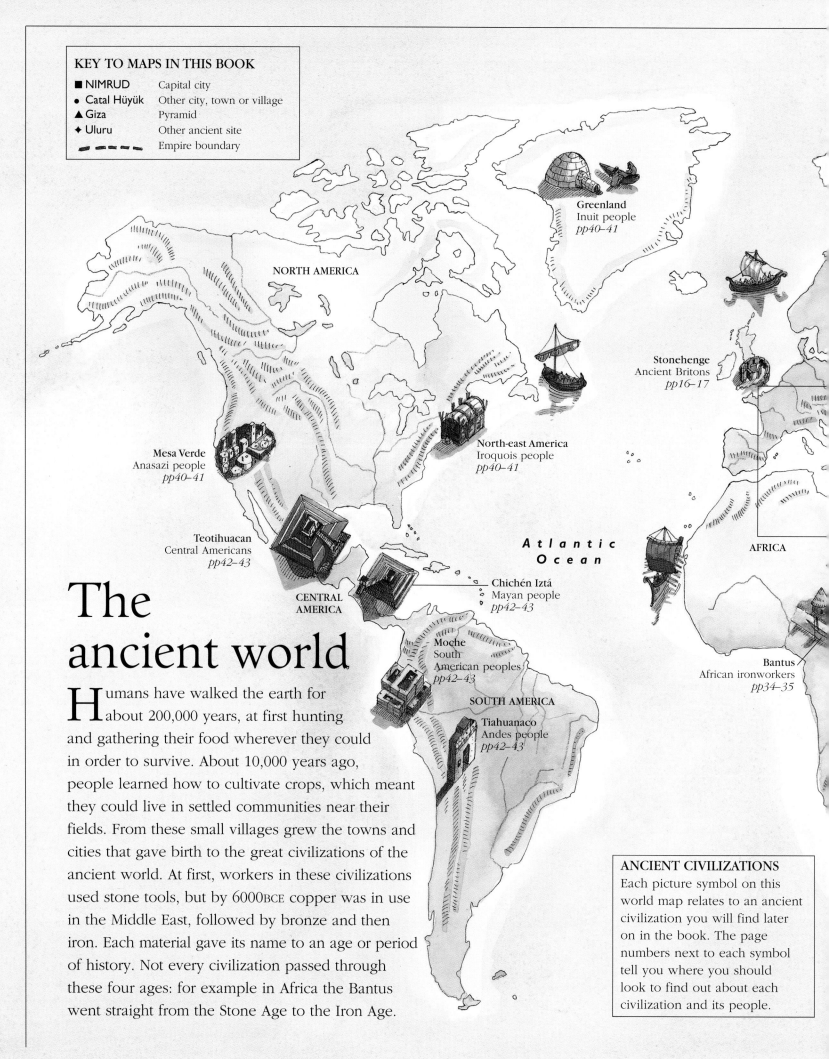

KEY TO MAPS IN THIS BOOK
- ■ NIMRUD   Capital city
- ● Catal Hüyük   Other city, town or village
- ▲ Giza   Pyramid
- ✦ Uluru   Other ancient site
- ▬ ▬ ▬ ▬   Empire boundary

NORTH AMERICA

Greenland
Inuit people
pp40–41

Stonehenge
Ancient Britons
pp16–17

Mesa Verde
Anasazi people
pp40–41

North-east America
Iroquois people
pp40–41

Teotihuacan
Central Americans
pp42–43

*Atlantic
Ocean*

AFRICA

CENTRAL
AMERICA

Chichén Iztá
Mayan people
pp42–43

Moche
South
American peoples
pp42–43

SOUTH AMERICA

Tiahuanaco
Andes people
pp42–43

Bantus
African ironworkers
pp34–35

The ancient world

Humans have walked the earth for about 200,000 years, at first hunting and gathering their food wherever they could in order to survive. About 10,000 years ago, people learned how to cultivate crops, which meant they could live in settled communities near their fields. From these small villages grew the towns and cities that gave birth to the great civilizations of the ancient world. At first, workers in these civilizations used stone tools, but by 6000BCE copper was in use in the Middle East, followed by bronze and then iron. Each material gave its name to an age or period of history. Not every civilization passed through these four ages: for example in Africa the Bantus went straight from the Stone Age to the Iron Age.

ANCIENT CIVILIZATIONS
Each picture symbol on this world map relates to an ancient civilization you will find later on in the book. The page numbers next to each symbol tell you where you should look to find out about each civilization and its people.

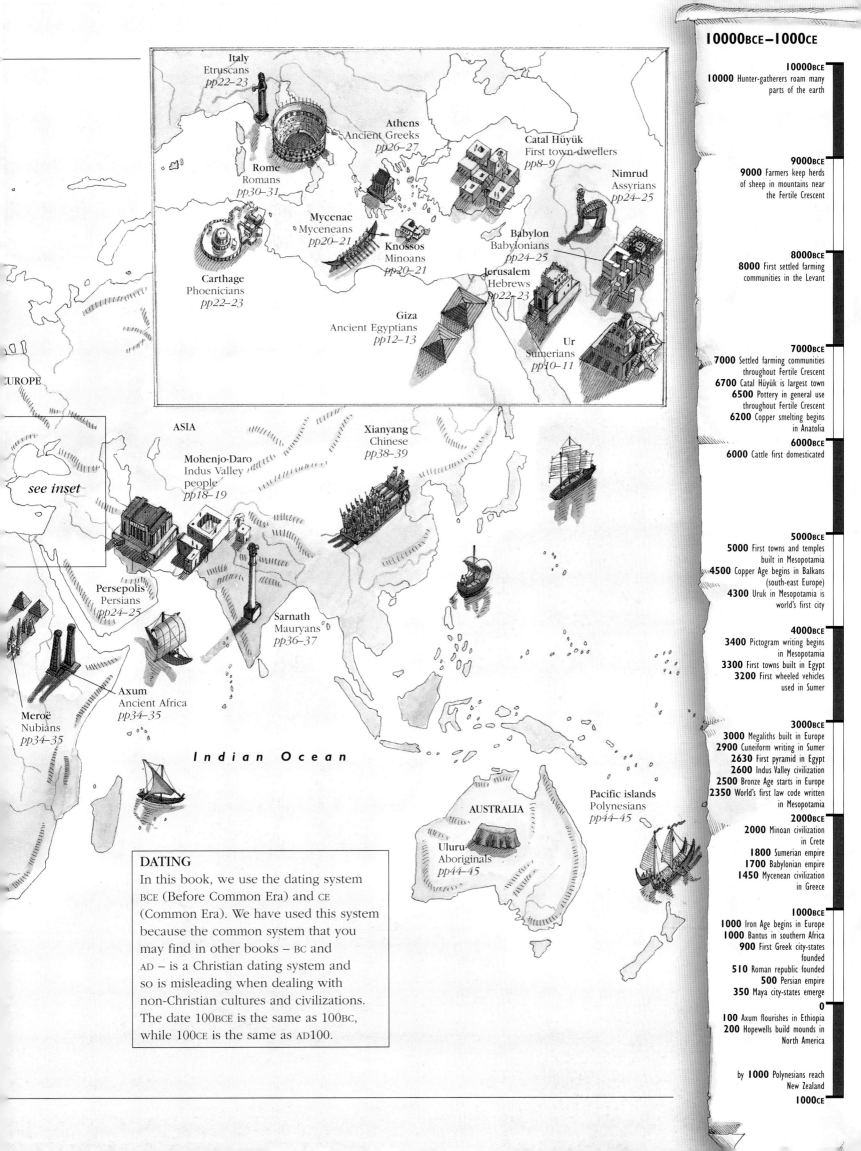

Italy
Etruscans
pp22–23

Athens
Ancient Greeks
pp26–27

Catal Hüyük
First town-dwellers
pp8–9

Nimrud
Assyrians
pp24–25

Rome
Romans
pp30–31

Mycenae
Myceneans
pp20–21

Knossos
Minoans
pp20–21

Babylon
Babylonians
pp24–25

Carthage
Phoenicians
pp22–23

Jerusalem
Hebrews
pp22–23

Giza
Ancient Egyptians
pp12–13

Ur
Sumerians
pp10–11

EUROPE

ASIA

Xianyang
Chinese
pp38–39

Mohenjo-Daro
Indus Valley
people
pp18–19

see inset

Persepolis
Persians
pp24–25

Sarnath
Mauryans
pp36–37

Axum
Ancient Africa
pp34–35

Meroë
Nubians
pp34–35

Indian Ocean

Pacific islands
Polynesians
pp44–45

AUSTRALIA

Uluru
Aboriginals
pp44–45

DATING

In this book, we use the dating system
BCE (Before Common Era) and CE
(Common Era). We have used this system
because the common system that you
may find in other books – BC and
AD – is a Christian dating system and
so is misleading when dealing with
non-Christian cultures and civilizations.
The date 100BCE is the same as 100BC,
while 100CE is the same as AD100.

10000BCE–1000CE

10000BCE
10000 Hunter-gatherers roam many
parts of the earth

9000BCE
9000 Farmers keep herds
of sheep in mountains near
the Fertile Crescent

8000BCE
8000 First settled farming
communities in the Levant

7000BCE
7000 Settled farming communities
throughout Fertile Crescent
6700 Catal Hüyük is largest town
6500 Pottery in general use
throughout Fertile Crescent
6200 Copper smelting begins
in Anatolia

6000BCE
6000 Cattle first domesticated

5000BCE
5000 First towns and temples
built in Mesopotamia
4500 Copper Age begins in Balkans
(south-east Europe)
4300 Uruk in Mesopotamia is
world's first city

4000BCE
3400 Pictogram writing begins
in Mesopotamia
3300 First towns built in Egypt
3200 First wheeled vehicles
used in Sumer

3000BCE
3000 Megaliths built in Europe
2900 Cuneiform writing in Sumer
2630 First pyramid in Egypt
2600 Indus Valley civilization
2500 Bronze Age starts in Europe
2350 World's first law code written
in Mesopotamia

2000BCE
2000 Minoan civilization
in Crete
1800 Sumerian empire
1700 Babylonian empire
1450 Mycenean civilization
in Greece

1000BCE
1000 Iron Age begins in Europe
1000 Bantus in southern Africa
900 First Greek city-states
founded
510 Roman republic founded
500 Persian empire
350 Maya city-states emerge

0
100 Axum flourishes in Ethiopia
200 Hopewells build mounds in
North America

by **1000** Polynesians reach
New Zealand

1000CE

The ancient world:
How we know about the past

Although we cannot travel back in time to speak to people who lived in the ancient world, we can discover much about them from the objects they left behind. Buildings, aqueducts and roads, everyday objects such as pots, tools, coins and writing implements, and luxury items such as jewellery and gold ornaments, have all survived to tell their tale. Some buildings, like the Forum in Rome, are still partly standing, while other buildings and smaller objects were buried for centuries and have only recently been uncovered by archaeologists. All these remains tell us a great deal about the peoples of the ancient world and the lives they led. From them we can piece together a picture of what it was like to live in ancient Rome or China, to march with Alexander's army or sail the Pacific colonizing new islands.

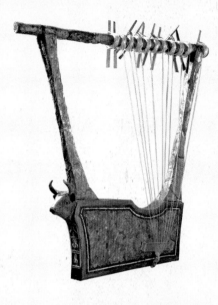

Royal music
This silver lyre – a stringed musical instrument – was made in Ur, southern Iraq, about 4,500 years ago. It was found in the Royal Cemetery, a lavish burial site where the kings of Ur were buried with their servants. Its fabulous craftsmanship and its place of discovery suggest that it was played at the royal court, and was buried with the king so that he could continue to enjoy it in the afterlife.

The Forum
The Forum was the political, judicial and commercial centre of Rome and the vast Roman Empire. Here senators met to discuss the big issues of the day and judges tried legal cases. Much of the Forum is now in ruins, but enough of its fine buildings, arches and monuments survive for us to see just how impressive it must have been when Rome and its armies dominated the western world.

Cuneiform writing

Priests in the cities of Sumer developed the world's first writing around 3400BCE. It consisted of simple pictures, each representing a word or idea. By 2900BCE, this had developed into cuneiform, a writing system using wedge-shaped marks (*cuneus* is Latin for wedge) made by pressing a reed stylus into wet clay.

Hieroglyphics

In about 3300BCE the ancient Egyptians began to use a form of writing known as hieroglyphics. These were more complex than Sumerian picture writing, using about 700 different signs to represent different ideas, words and even individual letters. The hieroglyphs above date from the 1st century BCE.

Mayan writing

Zapotec scribes in the Americas developed their own, unique form of hieroglyphic picture writing in about 800BCE. Later, the Maya used these to develop their own advanced literary language with a glyph for every syllable. Many glyphs have only recently been translated.

Hands-on history

Archaeologists study the evidence left behind by previous generations. They examine a site or object, looking for clues that might tell them how old it is, who made it, and why it was found where it was. Even the tiniest scrap of evidence can provide a vital clue, and archaeology can be a lengthy process. Here, an archaeologist is examining a Roman mosaic uncovered during road construction in Israel.

Chinese coins

We use coins every day, but each coin is a piece of history with a story of its own to tell. They show rulers and important symbols, and we can tell a lot about trade from where they are found. The Chinese have been using coins since the 5th century BCE. These were made with a hole in the middle so that they could be kept on a string.

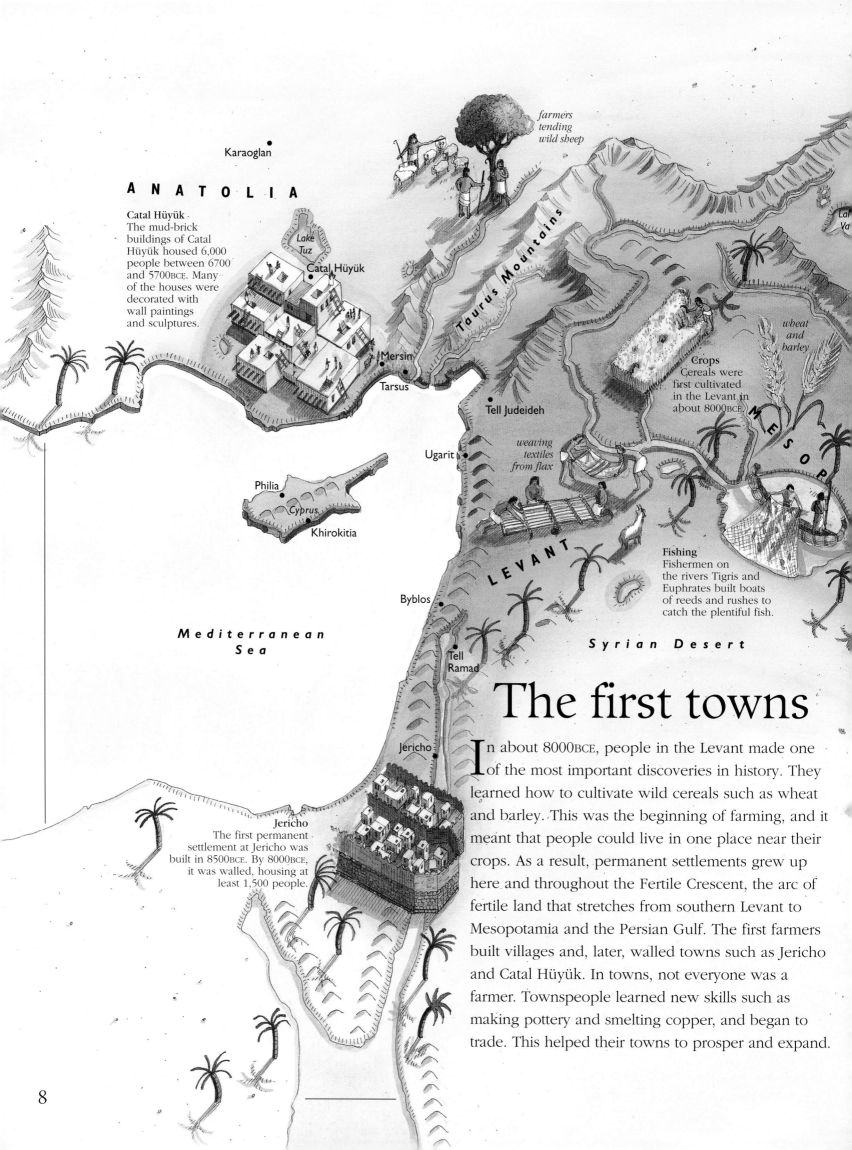

Karaoglan

A N A T O L I A

Catal Hüyük
The mud-brick buildings of Catal Hüyük housed 6,000 people between 6700 and 5700BCE. Many of the houses were decorated with wall paintings and sculptures.

farmers tending wild sheep

Lake Tuz

Catal Hüyük

Taurus Mountains

Mersin

Tarsus

Tell Judeideh

wheat and barley

Crops
Cereals were first cultivated in the Levant in about 8000BCE.

M E S O P

Ugarit

Philia

Cyprus

Khirokitia

weaving textiles from flax

L E V A N T

Fishing
Fishermen on the rivers Tigris and Euphrates built boats of reeds and rushes to catch the plentiful fish.

Byblos

Mediterranean Sea

Tell Ramad

S y r i a n   D e s e r t

The first towns

Jericho

Jericho
The first permanent settlement at Jericho was built in 8500BCE. By 8000BCE, it was walled, housing at least 1,500 people.

In about 8000BCE, people in the Levant made one of the most important discoveries in history. They learned how to cultivate wild cereals such as wheat and barley. This was the beginning of farming, and it meant that people could live in one place near their crops. As a result, permanent settlements grew up here and throughout the Fertile Crescent, the arc of fertile land that stretches from southern Levant to Mesopotamia and the Persian Gulf. The first farmers built villages and, later, walled towns such as Jericho and Catal Hüyük. In towns, not everyone was a farmer. Townspeople learned new skills such as making pottery and smelting copper, and began to trade. This helped their towns to prosper and expand.

ploughs helping farmers cultivate the land

Yanik Tepe

Lake Urmia

Pottery
The potters of Hassuna learned how to fire pottery in a kiln around 6000BCE.

Tepe Gawra

Hassuna
Tell Umm Dabaghiyeh

Smelting copper
Copper smelting to make weapons and tools reached southern Mesopotamia before 4000BCE.

Tigris

Samarra

Tell Al-Sawwan

Choga Mami

Irrigating the land
Farmers began building canals and irrigation ditches in Mesopotamia in about 5500BCE.

Tepe Guran

Tell Uqair

Nippur

Susa

Ali Kosh

Local industry
A pottery industry using local clay grew up in Susa and nearby towns in the 4000s BCE.

Euphrates

Uruk

Tel Awayli

Eridu

Zagros Mountains

Persian Gulf

The development of farming

The first peoples were hunter-gatherers who found food by killing wild animals and collecting wild fruits, nuts and cereals. In the Levant, wild crops were so plentiful that by about 10000BCE people did not need to move around to find food. Slowly they learned how to plant and grow wild cereals, so the crops would produce more food and be easier to harvest. Early farmers domesticated sheep, goats, pigs and cattle, so that by 6000BCE, they could feed a large, settled urban population.

Temples
The people of southern Mesopotamia built large temples and grain storehouses in Uruk and other towns after 5000BCE.

Eridu
Eridu, the oldest town in southern Mesopotamia, had a population of about 5,000 in 4000BCE. It traded pottery and other goods with Arabia.

0 ————— 200 km
0 ————— 100 miles

10000BCE
10000 Farmers in the Levant first build wooden huts with stone foundations

9500BCE

9000BCE
9000 Wild sheep herds are first kept by farmers in Taurus and Zagros Mountains

8500BCE

8000BCE
8000 Barley and wheat are cultivated in the Levant, allowing settled farming communities to develop
8000 Walled city of Jericho has 1,500 inhabitants

7500BCE
7500 Flax is first used for textiles

7000BCE
7000 Settled farming communities flourish throughout Fertile Crescent
7000 Goats, sheep and later pigs are domesticated in Taurus Mountains
6700 Catal Hüyük, with 6,000 inhabitants, is the largest town

6500BCE
6500 Pottery comes into general use

6200 Copper smelting begins in Catal Hüyük

6000BCE
6000 Cattle are first domesticated
6000 Kiln-fired pottery develops at Hassuna

5500BCE
5500 Irrigation allows farming communities to flourish in the arid soil of Mesopotamia

5000BCE
5000 The first towns and temples are built in Mesopotamia

4500BCE
4500 The plough, sail and potter's wheel are in common use in Mesopotamia
4300 Copper working for tools and weapons begins in Mesopotamia
4000 Sheep are bred for wool

4000BCE

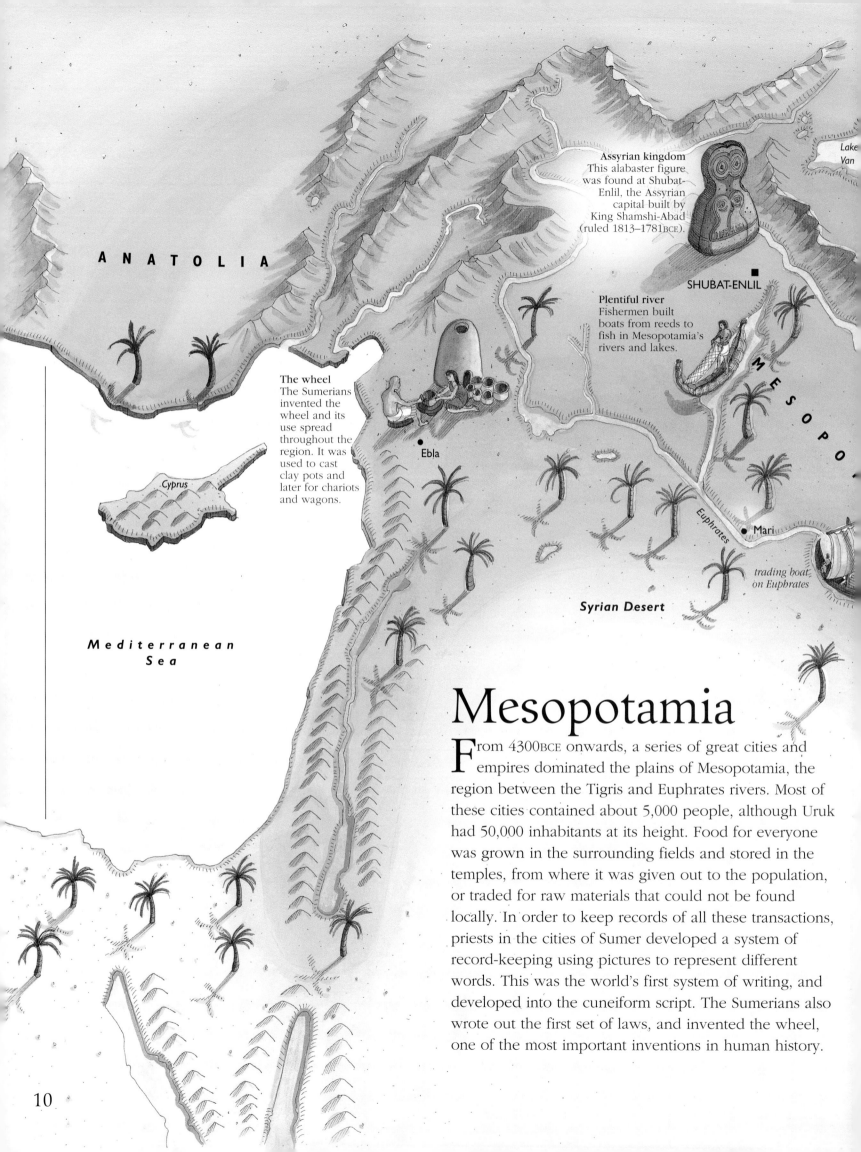

ANATOLIA

Assyrian kingdom
This alabaster figure was found at Shubat-Enlil, the Assyrian capital built by King Shamshi-Abad (ruled 1813–1781BCE).

SHUBAT-ENLIL

Lake Van

Plentiful river
Fishermen built boats from reeds to fish in Mesopotamia's rivers and lakes.

MESOPO.

The wheel
The Sumerians invented the wheel and its use spread throughout the region. It was used to cast clay pots and later for chariots and wagons.

• Ebla

Cyprus

Euphrates

• Mari

trading boat on Euphrates

Syrian Desert

Mediterranean Sea

Mesopotamia

From 4300BCE onwards, a series of great cities and empires dominated the plains of Mesopotamia, the region between the Tigris and Euphrates rivers. Most of these cities contained about 5,000 people, although Uruk had 50,000 inhabitants at its height. Food for everyone was grown in the surrounding fields and stored in the temples, from where it was given out to the population, or traded for raw materials that could not be found locally. In order to keep records of all these transactions, priests in the cities of Sumer developed a system of record-keeping using pictures to represent different words. This was the world's first system of writing, and developed into the cuneiform script. The Sumerians also wrote out the first set of laws, and invented the wheel, one of the most important inventions in human history.

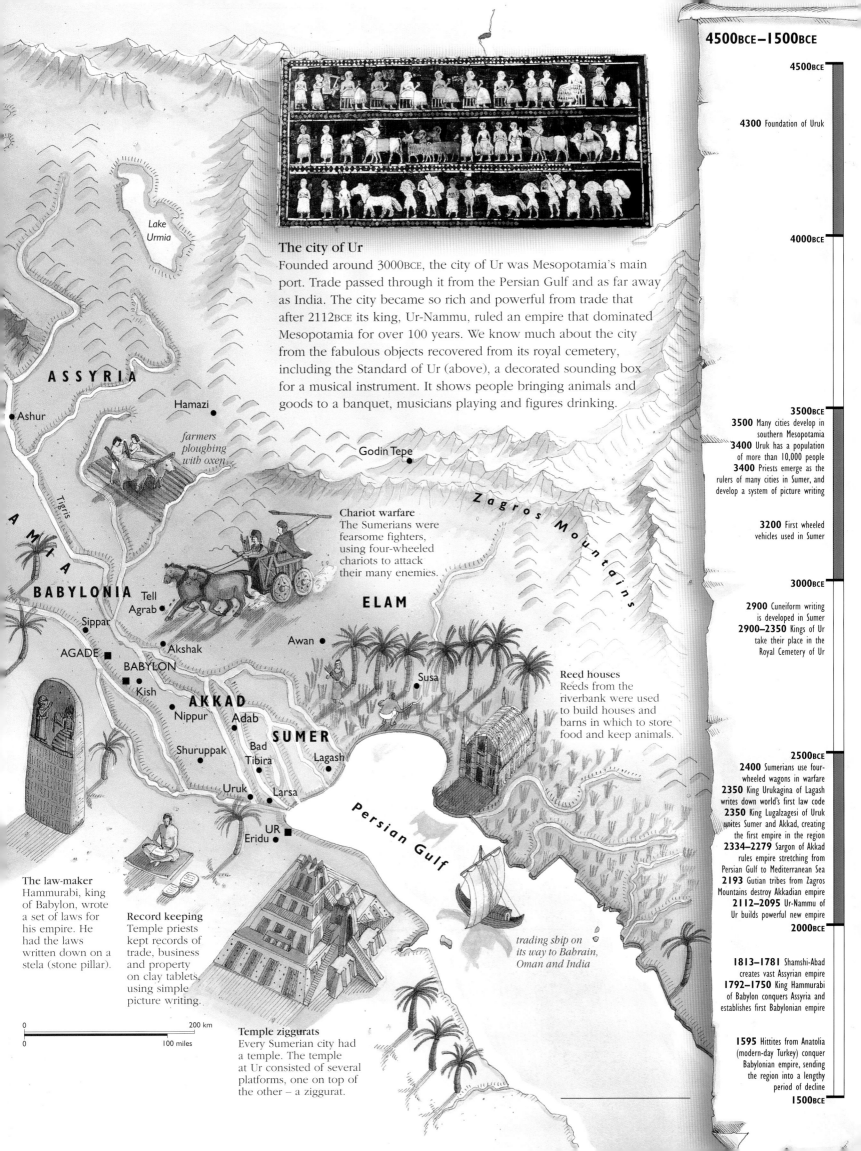

The city of Ur

Founded around 3000BCE, the city of Ur was Mesopotamia's main port. Trade passed through it from the Persian Gulf and as far away as India. The city became so rich and powerful from trade that after 2112BCE its king, Ur-Nammu, ruled an empire that dominated Mesopotamia for over 100 years. We know much about the city from the fabulous objects recovered from its royal cemetery, including the Standard of Ur (above), a decorated sounding box for a musical instrument. It shows people bringing animals and goods to a banquet, musicians playing and figures drinking.

farmers ploughing with oxen

Chariot warfare

The Sumerians were fearsome fighters, using four-wheeled chariots to attack their many enemies.

Reed houses

Reeds from the riverbank were used to build houses and barns in which to store food and keep animals.

The law-maker

Hammurabi, king of Babylon, wrote a set of laws for his empire. He had the laws written down on a stela (stone pillar).

Record keeping

Temple priests kept records of trade, business and property on clay tablets, using simple picture writing.

trading ship on its way to Bahrain, Oman and India

Temple ziggurats

Every Sumerian city had a temple. The temple at Ur consisted of several platforms, one on top of the other – a ziggurat.

Lake Urmia

ASSYRIA

Ashur
Hamazi
Godin Tepe

Zagros Mountains

Tigris

MITANNI

BABYLONIA
Tell Agrab
Sippar
AGADE
BABYLON
Kish

ELAM
Awan
Susa

AKKAD
Nippur
Adab
SUMER
Shuruppak
Bad Tibira
Lagash
Uruk
Larsa
UR
Eridu

Persian Gulf

| 0 | | 200 km |
| 0 | | 100 miles |

Ancient Egypt

For more than 3,000 years, the Egyptians established a remarkable civilization along the banks of the river Nile. They were ruled by kings called pharaohs. The river was Egypt's main highway. People and goods travelled along it and it supplied fresh water for humans and animals and irrigated the crops. Surplus food, linen and papyrus were traded throughout the region in return for silver, copper, tin, timber, horses and human slaves, making Egypt a wealthy and powerful nation. The Egyptians were one of the first people to invent a system of picture writing, known as hieroglyphics. They were also skilled builders, constructing magnificent stone palaces, temples and pyramid-shaped tombs, many of which still survive today.

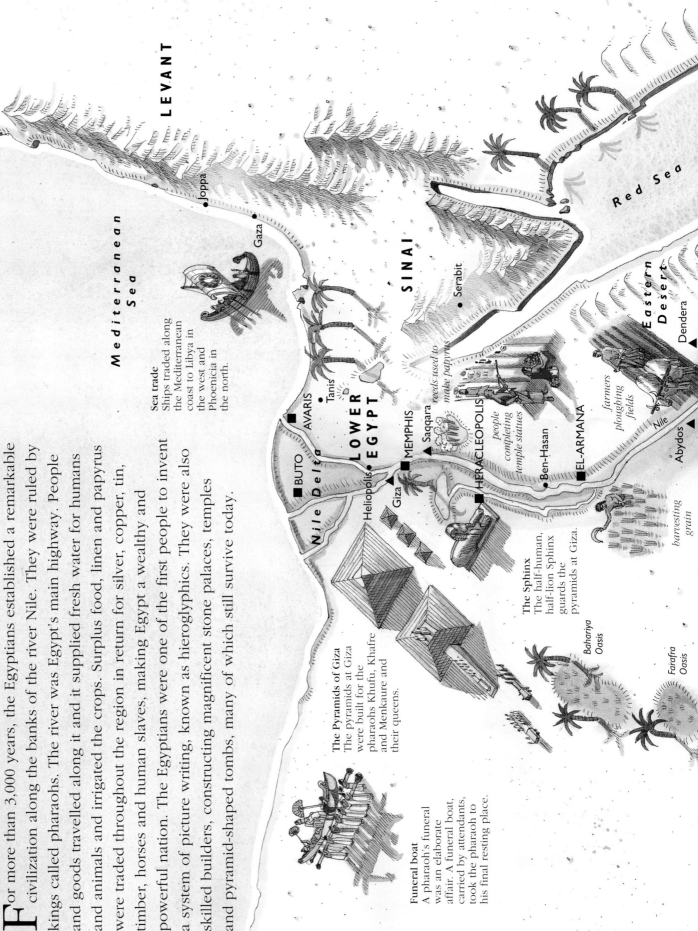

LEVANT

Mediterranean Sea

Joppa

Gaza

Sea trade
Ships traded along the Mediterranean coast to Libya in the west and Phoenicia in the north.

SINAI

Serabit

Red Sea

Eastern Desert

Dendera

BUTO

AVARIS

Tanis

LOWER EGYPT

Nile Delta

Heliopolis

MEMPHIS

Giza

Saqqara

HERACLEOPOLIS

reeds used to make papyrus

people completing temple statues

Ben-Hasan

EL-ARMANA

farmers ploughing fields

Nile

Abydos

harvesting grain

The Sphinx
The half-human, half-lion Sphinx guards the Pyramids at Giza.

Bahariya Oasis

Farafra Oasis

The Pyramids of Giza
The pyramids at Giza were built for the pharaohs Khufu, Khafre and Menkaure and their queens.

Funeral boat
A pharaoh's funeral was an elaborate affair. A funeral boat, carried by attendants, took the pharaoh to his final resting place.

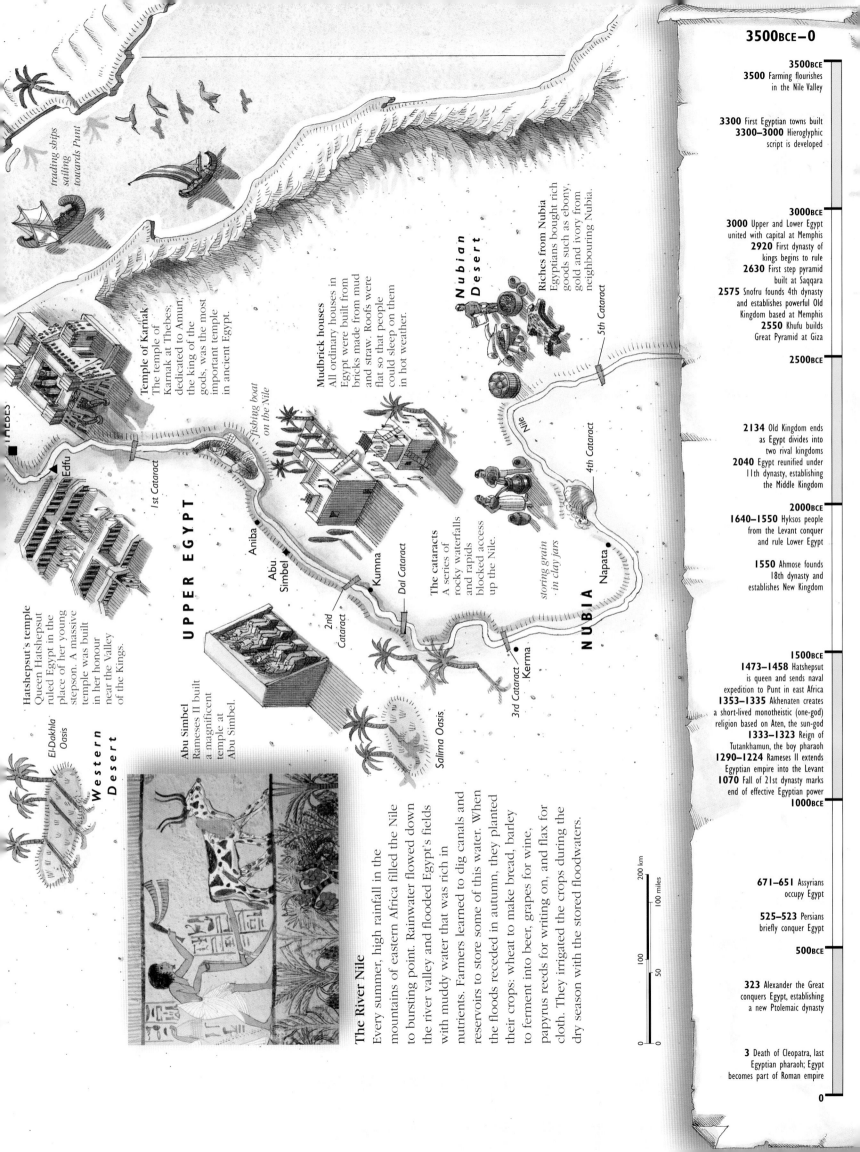

trading ships sailing towards Punt

Temple of Karnak
The temple of Karnak at Thebes, dedicated to Amun, the king of the gods, was the most important temple in ancient Egypt.

Mudbrick houses
All ordinary houses in Egypt were built from bricks made from mud and straw. Roofs were flat so that people could sleep on them in hot weather.

Riches from Nubia
Egyptians bought rich goods such as ebony, gold and ivory from neighbouring Nubia.

Nubian Desert

fishing boat on the Nile

5th Cataract

Nile

4th Cataract

The cataracts
A series of rocky waterfalls and rapids blocked access up the Nile.

storing grain in clay jars

THEBES

Edfu

1st Cataract

UPPER EGYPT

Aniba

Abu Simbel

Kumna

Dal Cataract

2nd Cataract

Napata

NUBIA

Kerma

3rd Cataract

Salima Oasis

Hatshepsut's temple
Queen Hatshepsut ruled Egypt in the place of her young stepson. A massive temple was built in her honour near the Valley of the Kings.

El-Dakhla Oasis

Western Desert

Abu Simbel
Rameses II built a magnificent temple at Abu Simbel.

The River Nile

Every summer, high rainfall in the mountains of eastern Africa filled the Nile to bursting point. Rainwater flowed down the river valley and flooded Egypt's fields with muddy water that was rich in nutrients. Farmers learned to dig canals and reservoirs to store some of this water. When the floods receded in autumn, they planted their crops: wheat to make bread, barley to ferment into beer, grapes for wine, papyrus reeds for writing on, and flax for cloth. They irrigated the crops during the dry season with the stored floodwaters.

200 km

100 miles

100

50

3500BCE

3500 Farming flourishes in the Nile Valley

3300 First Egyptian towns built
3300–3000 Hieroglyphic script is developed

3000BCE

3000 Upper and Lower Egypt united with capital at Memphis
2920 First dynasty of kings begins to rule
2630 First step pyramid built at Saqqara
2575 Snofru founds 4th dynasty and establishes powerful Old Kingdom based at Memphis
2550 Khufu builds Great Pyramid at Giza

2500BCE

2134 Old Kingdom ends as Egypt divides into two rival kingdoms
2040 Egypt reunified under 11th dynasty, establishing the Middle Kingdom

2000BCE
1640–1550 Hyksos people from the Levant conquer and rule Lower Egypt

1550 Ahmose founds 18th dynasty and establishes New Kingdom

1500BCE
1473–1458 Hatshepsut is queen and sends naval expedition to Punt in east Africa
1353–1335 Akhenaten creates a short-lived monotheistic (one-god) religion based on Aten, the sun-god
1333–1323 Reign of Tutankhamun, the boy pharaoh
1290–1224 Rameses II extends Egyptian empire into the Levant
1070 Fall of 21st dynasty marks end of effective Egyptian power

1000BCE

671–651 Assyrians occupy Egypt

525–523 Persians briefly conquer Egypt

500BCE

323 Alexander the Great conquers Egypt, establishing a new Ptolemaic dynasty

3 Death of Cleopatra, last Egyptian pharaoh; Egypt becomes part of Roman empire

0

Ancient Egypt:
Preparing for the afterlife

The ancient Egyptians had a strong belief in the afterlife, as they dreaded the day their own world might come to an end. They developed an elaborate method of embalming and mummifying bodies so that they would last for ever. Important people, such as the pharaoh (king), were buried along with their belongings inside a great pyramid. Later, the pharaohs were buried in tombs in the Valley of the Kings. Although most of these pyramids and tombs have been robbed of their contents, a few have survived intact, giving us a good idea about the Egyptian way of life and death, 3,000 and more years ago.

Mummification

After death, the body was taken to a place known as the Beautiful House to be preserved. Embalmers removed the internal organs, leaving the heart so that it could be weighed in the afterlife. The body was then covered with crystals of a chemical called natron, to dry it out and prevent decay. After about 40 days, the body was ready for the next stage. It was stuffed with dry material such as sawdust or leaves and wrapped tightly in linen bandages. Lastly, it was put into a wood or stone coffin. Lowly people were buried in graveyards, but important people, such as the boy pharaoh Tutankhamun (right; ruled 1333–1323BCE) were placed in an elaborate container. This was made up of layers, each one beautifully decorated inside with gods of the underworld, and outside with hieroglyphs and magic symbols. Once safely in its coffin, the body was ready for the afterlife.

Weighing the heart

The Egyptians believed in an underworld called Duat, which contained lakes of fire and poisonous snakes. Spells to ward off these and other dangers were written on the coffin. The biggest danger was in the Hall of Two Truths, where a person's heart was weighed against past deeds (left). Here the dead person was asked about their life. If they told the truth, they were allowed to pass on into the afterlife.

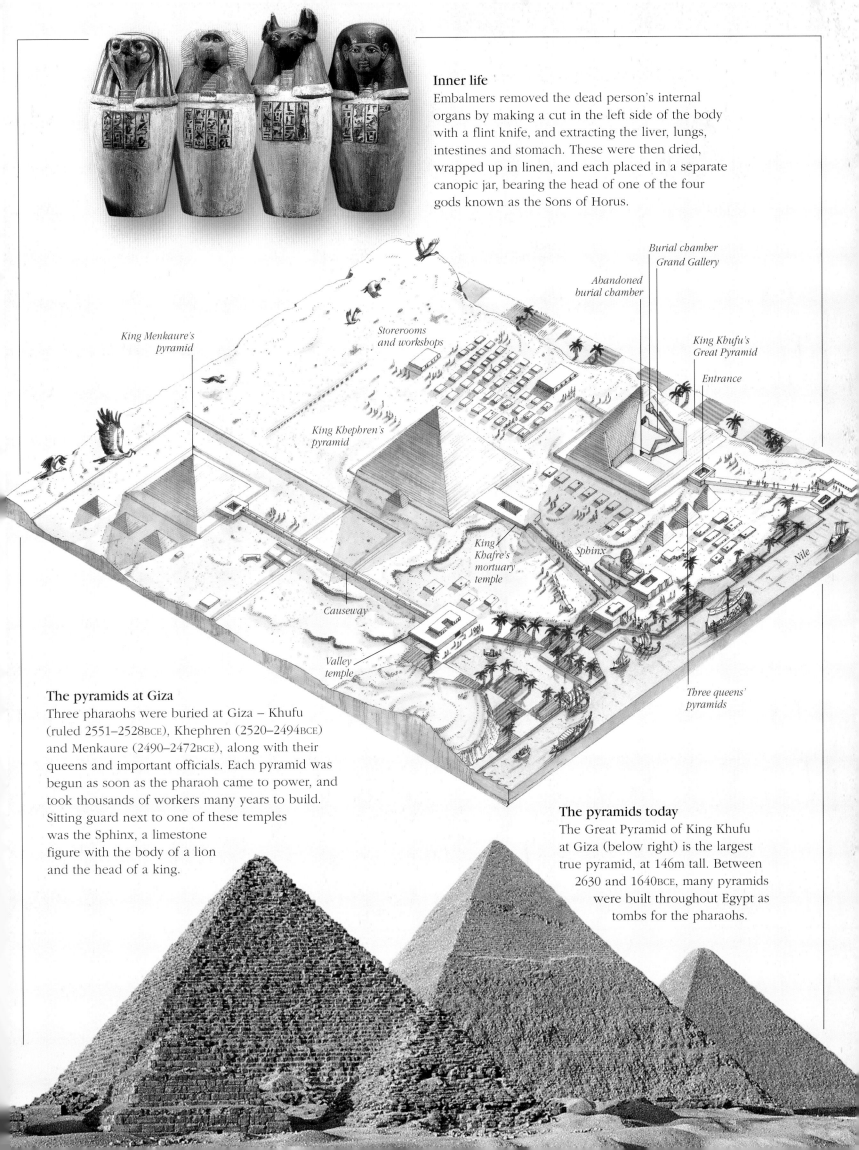

Inner life

Embalmers removed the dead person's internal organs by making a cut in the left side of the body with a flint knife, and extracting the liver, lungs, intestines and stomach. These were then dried, wrapped up in linen, and each placed in a separate canopic jar, bearing the head of one of the four gods known as the Sons of Horus.

Burial chamber
Grand Gallery

Abandoned burial chamber

King Khufu's Great Pyramid

Entrance

King Menkaure's pyramid

Storerooms and workshops

King Khephren's pyramid

King Khafre's mortuary temple

Sphinx

Nile

Causeway

Valley temple

Three queens' pyramids

The pyramids at Giza

Three pharaohs were buried at Giza – Khufu (ruled 2551–2528BCE), Khephren (2520–2494BCE) and Menkaure (2490–2472BCE), along with their queens and important officials. Each pyramid was begun as soon as the pharaoh came to power, and took thousands of workers many years to build. Sitting guard next to one of these temples was the Sphinx, a limestone figure with the body of a lion and the head of a king.

The pyramids today

The Great Pyramid of King Khufu at Giza (below right) is the largest true pyramid, at 146m tall. Between 2630 and 1640BCE, many pyramids were built throughout Egypt as tombs for the pharaohs.

Ancient Europe

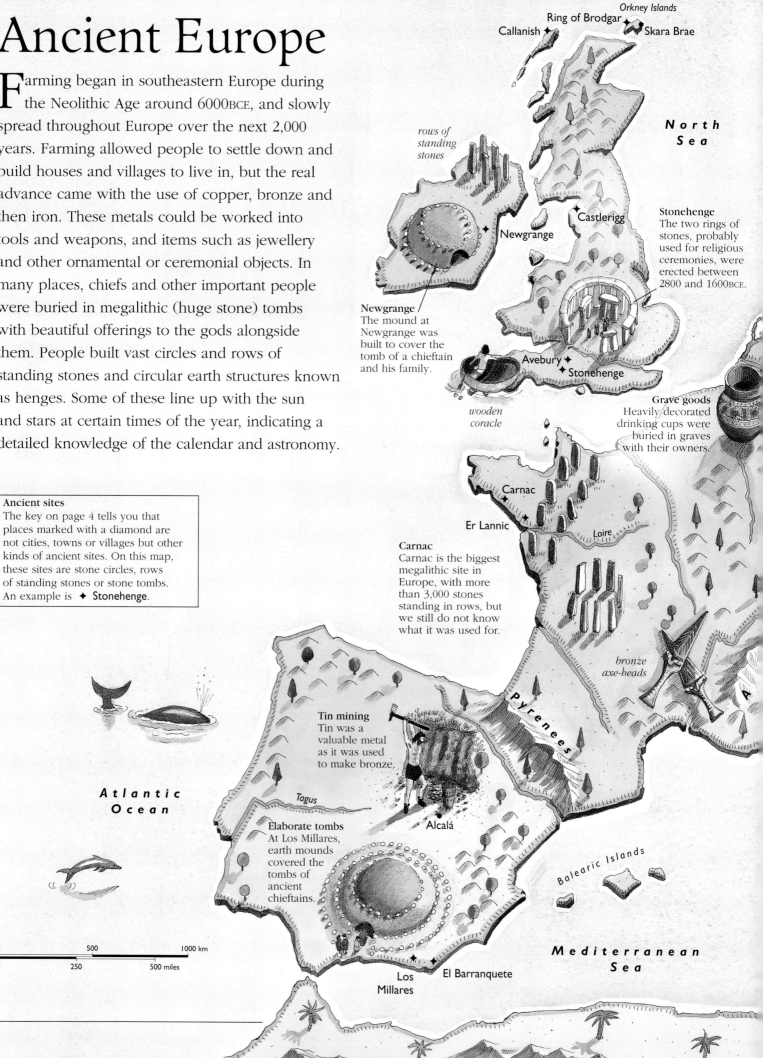

Farming began in southeastern Europe during the Neolithic Age around 6000BCE, and slowly spread throughout Europe over the next 2,000 years. Farming allowed people to settle down and build houses and villages to live in, but the real advance came with the use of copper, bronze and then iron. These metals could be worked into tools and weapons, and items such as jewellery and other ornamental or ceremonial objects. In many places, chiefs and other important people were buried in megalithic (huge stone) tombs with beautiful offerings to the gods alongside them. People built vast circles and rows of standing stones and circular earth structures known as henges. Some of these line up with the sun and stars at certain times of the year, indicating a detailed knowledge of the calendar and astronomy.

Ancient sites
The key on page 4 tells you that places marked with a diamond are not cities, towns or villages but other kinds of ancient sites. On this map, these sites are stone circles, rows of standing stones or stone tombs. An example is ✦ Stonehenge.

rows of standing stones

North Sea

Orkney Islands
Ring of Brodgar
Callanish ✦
Skara Brae

Castlerigg

Stonehenge
The two rings of stones, probably used for religious ceremonies, were erected between 2800 and 1600BCE.

Newgrange

Newgrange
The mound at Newgrange was built to cover the tomb of a chieftain and his family.

Avebury ✦
✦ Stonehenge

wooden coracle

Grave goods
Heavily decorated drinking cups were buried in graves with their owners.

Carnac

Er Lannic

Loire

Carnac
Carnac is the biggest megalithic site in Europe, with more than 3,000 stones standing in rows, but we still do not know what it was used for.

bronze axe-heads

Pyrenees

Tin mining
Tin was a valuable metal as it was used to make bronze.

Tagus

Alcalá

Elaborate tombs
At Los Millares, earth mounds covered the tombs of ancient chieftains.

Atlantic Ocean

Balearic Islands

Mediterranean Sea

Los Millares

El Barranquete

0	500	1000 km
0	250	500 miles

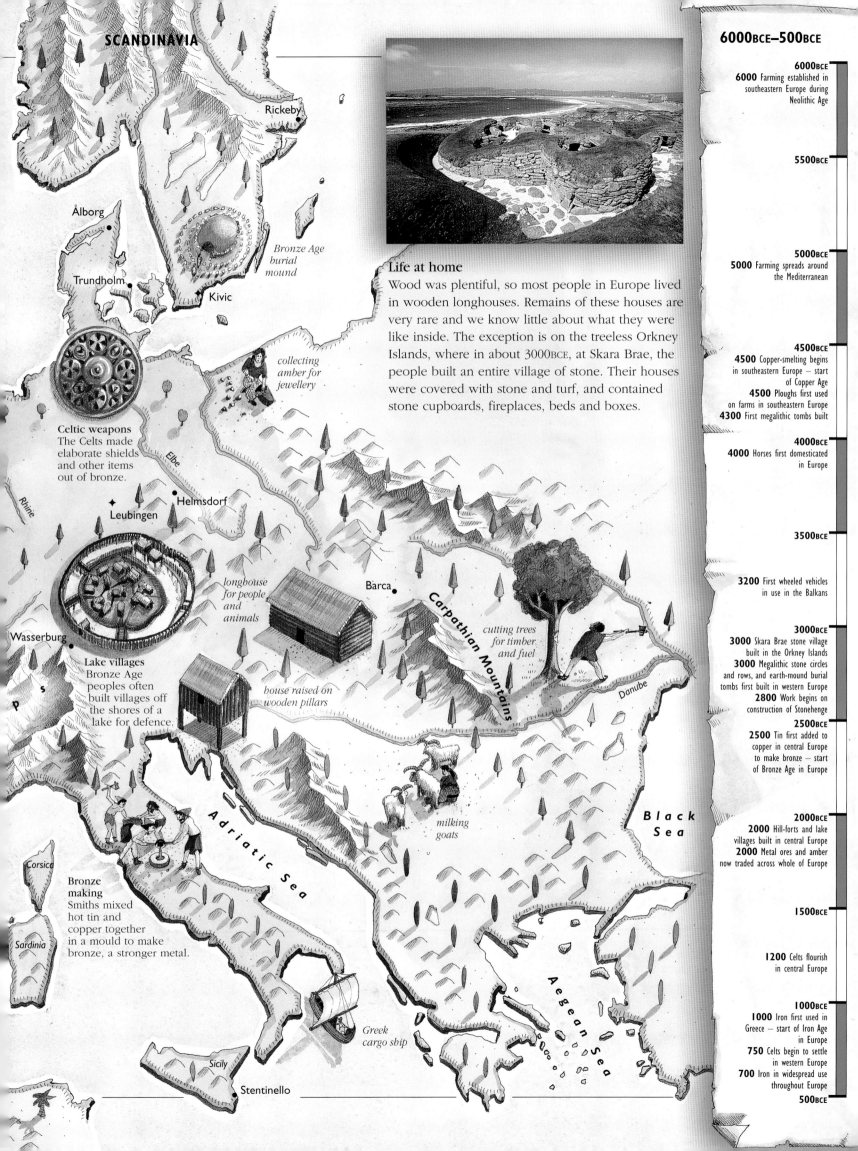

SCANDINAVIA

Rickeby

Ålborg

Trundholm

Kivic

Bronze Age burial mound

Celtic weapons
The Celts made elaborate shields and other items out of bronze.

collecting amber for jewellery

Elbe

Rhine

Leubingen

Helmsdorf

Lake villages
Bronze Age peoples often built villages off the shores of a lake for defence.

Wasserburg

A l p s

Barca

longhouse for people and animals

house raised on wooden pillars

Carpathian Mountains

cutting trees for timber and fuel

Danube

milking goats

B l a c k   S e a

Corsica

Bronze making
Smiths mixed hot tin and copper together in a mould to make bronze, a stronger metal.

Sardinia

A d r i a t i c   S e a

Greek cargo ship

A e g e a n   S e a

Sicily

Stentinello

Life at home
Wood was plentiful, so most people in Europe lived in wooden longhouses. Remains of these houses are very rare and we know little about what they were like inside. The exception is on the treeless Orkney Islands, where in about 3000BCE, at Skara Brae, the people built an entire village of stone. Their houses were covered with stone and turf, and contained stone cupboards, fireplaces, beds and boxes.

6000BCE–500BCE

6000BCE
6000 Farming established in southeastern Europe during Neolithic Age

5500BCE

5000BCE
5000 Farming spreads around the Mediterranean

4500BCE
4500 Copper-smelting begins in southeastern Europe – start of Copper Age
4500 Ploughs first used on farms in southeastern Europe
4300 First megalithic tombs built

4000BCE
4000 Horses first domesticated in Europe

3500BCE

3200 First wheeled vehicles in use in the Balkans

3000BCE
3000 Skara Brae stone village built in the Orkney Islands
3000 Megalithic stone circles and rows, and earth-mound burial tombs first built in western Europe
2800 Work begins on construction of Stonehenge

2500BCE
2500 Tin first added to copper in central Europe to make bronze – start of Bronze Age in Europe

2000BCE
2000 Hill-forts and lake villages built in central Europe
2000 Metal ores and amber now traded across whole of Europe

1500BCE

1200 Celts flourish in central Europe

1000BCE
1000 Iron first used in Greece – start of Iron Age in Europe
750 Celts begin to settle in western Europe
700 Iron in widespread use throughout Europe

500BCE

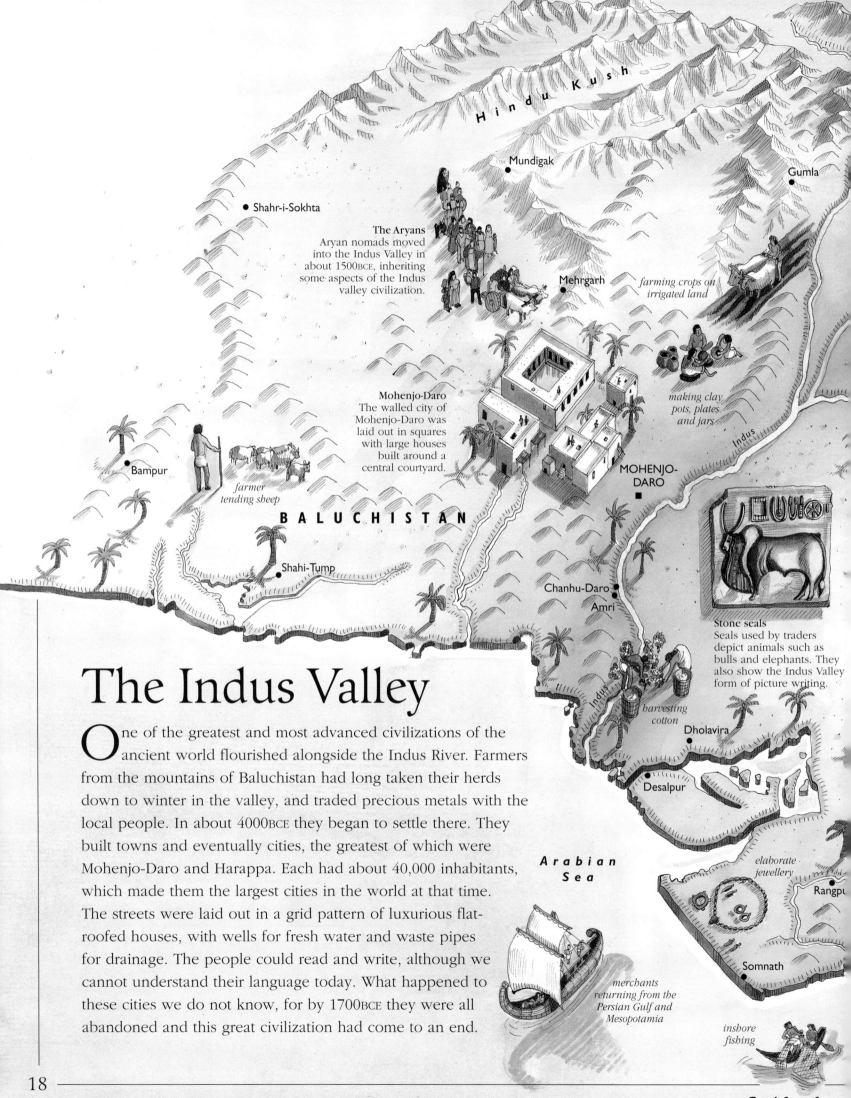

Gumla

Mundigak

Shahr-i-Sokhta

The Aryans
Aryan nomads moved into the Indus Valley in about 1500BCE, inheriting some aspects of the Indus valley civilization.

Mehrgarh

farming crops on irrigated land

Mohenjo-Daro
The walled city of Mohenjo-Daro was laid out in squares with large houses built around a central courtyard.

making clay pots, plates and jars

Bampur

farmer tending sheep

B A L U C H I S T A N

MOHENJO-DARO

Shahi-Tump

Chanhu-Daro

Amri

Stone seals
Seals used by traders depict animals such as bulls and elephants. They also show the Indus Valley form of picture writing.

harvesting cotton

Dholavira

Desalpur

The Indus Valley

One of the greatest and most advanced civilizations of the ancient world flourished alongside the Indus River. Farmers from the mountains of Baluchistan had long taken their herds down to winter in the valley, and traded precious metals with the local people. In about 4000BCE they began to settle there. They built towns and eventually cities, the greatest of which were Mohenjo-Daro and Harappa. Each had about 40,000 inhabitants, which made them the largest cities in the world at that time. The streets were laid out in a grid pattern of luxurious flat-roofed houses, with wells for fresh water and waste pipes for drainage. The people could read and write, although we cannot understand their language today. What happened to these cities we do not know, for by 1700BCE they were all abandoned and this great civilization had come to an end.

*A r a b i a n
S e a*

elaborate jewellery

Rangpu

merchants returning from the Persian Gulf and Mesopotamia

Somnath

inshore fishing

*Gulf of
Khabhat*

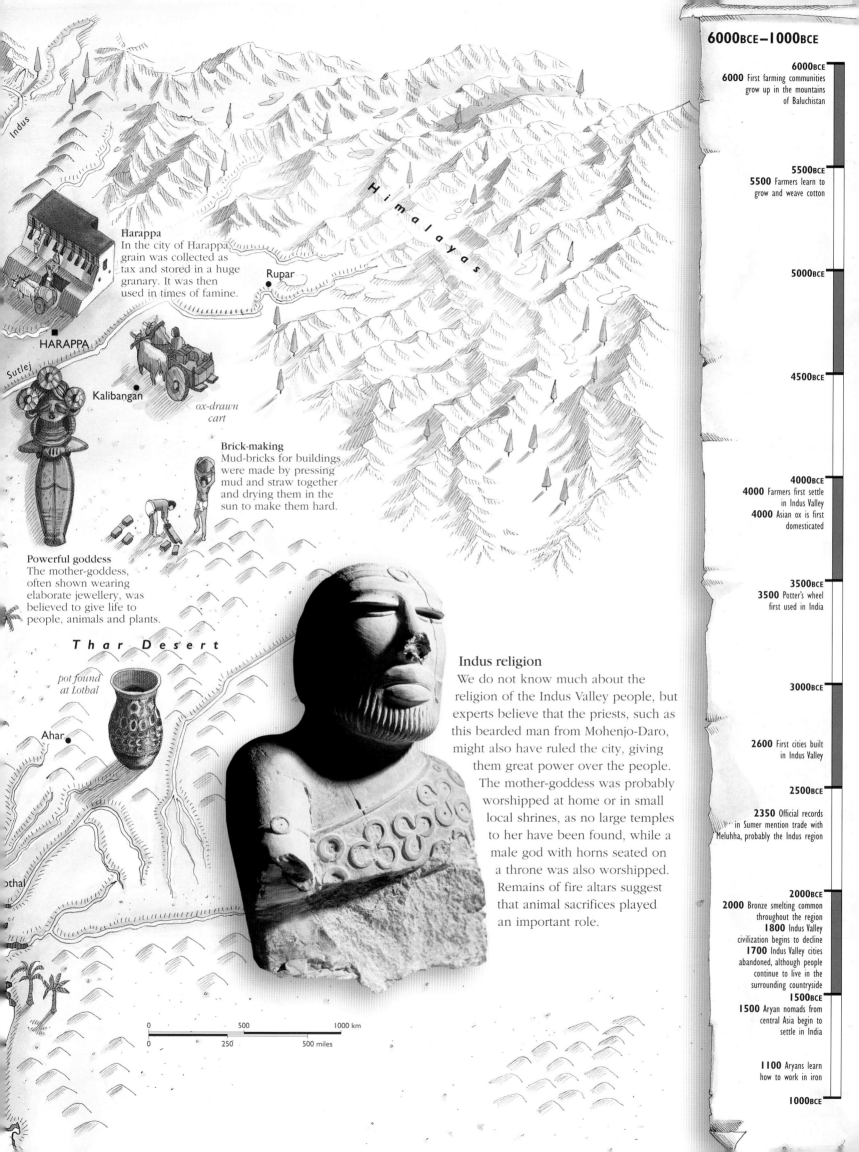

Harappa
In the city of Harappa, grain was collected as tax and stored in a huge granary. It was then used in times of famine.

Rupar

HARAPPA

Sutlej

Kalibangan

ox-drawn cart

Brick-making
Mud-bricks for buildings were made by pressing mud and straw together and drying them in the sun to make them hard.

Powerful goddess
The mother-goddess, often shown wearing elaborate jewellery, was believed to give life to people, animals and plants.

Thar Desert

pot found at Lothal

Ahar

Lothal

Indus

Himalayas

Indus religion

We do not know much about the religion of the Indus Valley people, but experts believe that the priests, such as this bearded man from Mohenjo-Daro, might also have ruled the city, giving them great power over the people. The mother-goddess was probably worshipped at home or in small local shrines, as no large temples to her have been found, while a male god with horns seated on a throne was also worshipped. Remains of fire altars suggest that animal sacrifices played an important role.

0   500   1000 km
0   250   500 miles

6000BCE–1000BCE

6000BCE
6000 First farming communities grow up in the mountains of Baluchistan

5500BCE
5500 Farmers learn to grow and weave cotton

5000BCE

4500BCE

4000BCE
4000 Farmers first settle in Indus Valley
4000 Asian ox is first domesticated

3500BCE
3500 Potter's wheel first used in India

3000BCE

2600 First cities built in Indus Valley

2500BCE

2350 Official records in Sumer mention trade with Meluhha, probably the Indus region

2000BCE
2000 Bronze smelting common throughout the region
1800 Indus Valley civilization begins to decline
1700 Indus Valley cities abandoned, although people continue to live in the surrounding countryside

1500BCE
1500 Aryan nomads from central Asia begin to settle in India

1100 Aryans learn how to work in iron

1000BCE

olive
harvesting

Karditsa

Iolkos

Mycenae's Lion Gate
This magnificent
stone gate was the
main entrance to
the city and one
of the only ways
through its walls.

wheat
farming

Royal graves
Mycenean leaders
were buried in shaft
graves. The one at
Mycenae contained
bronze weapons
and rich goods.

Orchomenos   Gla

Chalcis

Lefkandi

Thebes

Dyme

Marathon

Athens

PELOPONNESE

Mycenae

Tiryns   Dendra

Minoans
and Myceneans

The Minoan civilization began on the island of Crete
over 4,000 years ago. By 2000BCE, the Minoans had
built several cities with impressive palaces. The capital,
Knossos, had the grandest palace complex, with temples,
storerooms, workshops and everything needed for daily life.
Riches from trade meant the Minoans were envied by the
neighbouring Myceneans. These people had migrated to
Greece from the Balkans in around 2000BCE. Their civilization
grew from a series of hillside villages to fortified city-states.
The two cultures lived side by side for some time, and both
developed forms of writing. In 1626BCE, a massive earthquake
caused by a volcanic eruption on Thera damaged the Minoan
cities. Shortly afterwards, Crete was invaded and colonized
by the Myceneans, and Mycenean civilization dominated the
region until it too was conquered in around 1200BCE.

Menelaion

Vapheio

Pylos

Height of power
Mycenean cities were
built on hilltops and
surrounded by strong
defensive walls.

Mycenean
warship bound
for Crete

Mycenean
trading ship
going to Sicily

wealthy
Minoan
people

Kha

Trojan horse
Agamemnon, the leader of the Greeks who conquered Troy, was almost certainly a Mycenean king.

Minoan trading ship

Aegean Sea

Lemnos
Poliochni
•Troy

Lesbos

Chios

Andros

Serraglia
Kos
Miletos•

Delos

ANATOLIA

merchants from Miletos trading with Hittites

Paros Naxos

elos
Phylakopi

volcano erupting on Thera

Thera

Ialysos

Rhodes
Lindos

Legendary beast
For the Minoans and Myceneans, the bull was a sacred symbol of power. This wall painting from the palace at Knossos shows the sport of bull-leaping. Athletes would vault over the animal's horns, symbolizing the mastering of its strength. Bulls were so important to Minoan life that their most famous legend is of the Minotaur, a terrible monster which was half man and half bull, and lived in an underground maze at Knossos.

Luxurious palace
The palace at Knossos had royal apartments, courtyards, underfloor heating, sunken baths, running water and lush gardens.

Knossos•
Phaistos• **CRETE**
•Zakros

0 ———— 100 ———— 200 km
0 —— 50 —— 100 miles

2000BCE
2000 Minoans begin to build cities and palaces on Crete, and create the first states in Europe
2000 Minoans develop their own hieroglyphic (picture) script
2000 Greek-speaking Myceneans move south from the Balkans to settle in Greece

1900BCE

1800BCE

1700BCE
1700 After a big fire, possibly caused by warfare, Minoan palaces are rebuilt; Knossos becomes main city
1650 Myceneans build fortified towns in mainland Greece and begin to create small kingdoms
1626 Volcano erupts at Thera; earthquakes and ash falls engulf Crete

1600BCE
1600 Myceneans begin to bury their dead leaders in shaft graves

1500BCE
1450 Myceneans conquer Crete and end Minoan civilization
1450 Myceneans begin to settle in colonies such as Miletos on the Anatolian coast
1450 Myceneans develop Linear B script, the origin of modern-day Greek writing

1400BCE

1300BCE
1250 City of Troy is twice attacked around this time, giving rise to the Greek legend of the Trojan wars

1200BCE
1200 Sea Peoples from Anatolia attack Greece and end Mycenean civilization; many Myceneans move to Anatolia and Cyprus

1100BCE
1100 Greek-speaking Dorians move south from Balkans to settle in Greece

1000BCE

BRITAIN

Hannibal
In 218BCE the Carthaginian general Hannibal crossed the Alps to surprise his Roman enemies during the Second Punic War.

Phoenician ship sailing to Britain to get tin

A t l a n t i c   O c e a n

FRANCE

tin mining

P y r e n e e s

A L P S

ITALY

Massilia

The Etruscans
The Etruscans – the major force in central Italy – ruled Rome before it became a republic in 509BCE.

Corsica

silver mining

SPAIN

M e d i t e r r a n e a n   S e a

Palma

Balearic Islands

Sardinia

Sulcis

ROME

A d r i a t i c   S e a

Rome
Rome was originally a series of hilltop villages that gradually joined to become a single city.

Gades

Cartagena

Tingis (Tangier)

trading prized Phoenician cloth

Lixus

Cartenna

Sicily

CARTHAGE

trading ship travelling along African coast

Carthage harbour
The Phoenicians established the trading post of Carthage in 814BCE. It soon grew to become the most powerful nation in the Mediterranean.

Peoples of the Mediterranean

Phoenician script
The Phoenicians had an alphabet of 22 consonants. The Greeks added vowels, making the alphabet we use today.

For the people living near the Mediterranean, the sea presented either a barrier they could not cross or a wonderful opportunity to get rich through trade and conquest. The Greeks established trading colonies around the Mediterranean, while the Phoenicians were more adventurous and sent trading expeditions out into the Atlantic. The two peoples often fought. They were later joined by the Carthaginians in North Africa, the Etruscans from Italy and, eventually, the Romans, who dominated the Mediterranean Sea and much of its coastline by 100BCE.

Human sacrifice
The Carthaginians worshipped the sun and moon gods, offering human sacrifices in times of danger.

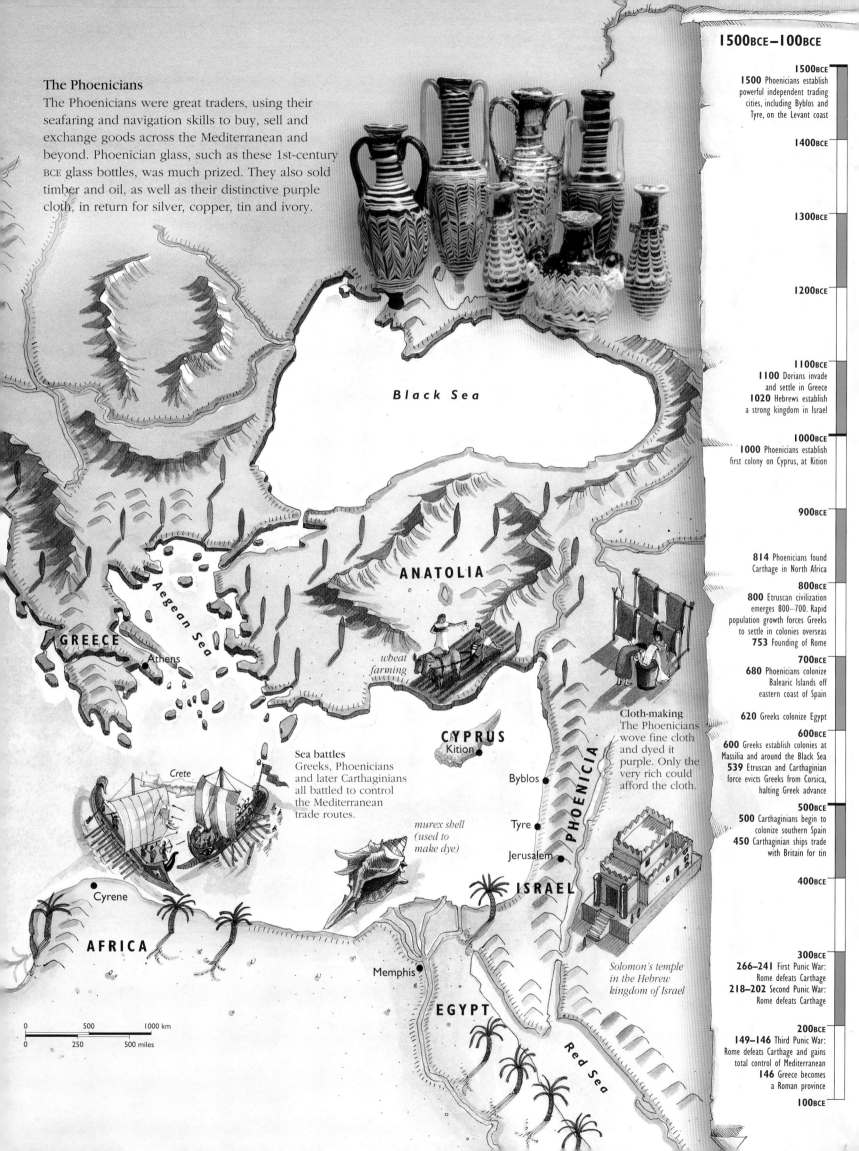

The Phoenicians

The Phoenicians were great traders, using their seafaring and navigation skills to buy, sell and exchange goods across the Mediterranean and beyond. Phoenician glass, such as these 1st-century BCE glass bottles, was much prized. They also sold timber and oil, as well as their distinctive purple cloth, in return for silver, copper, tin and ivory.

Black Sea

ANATOLIA

wheat farming

GREECE

Aegean Sea

Athens

CYPRUS
Kition

Cloth-making
The Phoenicians wove fine cloth and dyed it purple. Only the very rich could afford the cloth.

Sea battles
Greeks, Phoenicians and later Carthaginians all battled to control the Mediterranean trade routes.

Crete

Byblos

murex shell (used to make dye)

Tyre

P H O E N I C I A

Jerusalem

ISRAEL

Cyrene

AFRICA

Solomon's temple in the Hebrew kingdom of Israel

Memphis

EGYPT

Red Sea

| 0 | 500 | 1000 km |
| 0 | 250 | 500 miles |

Black Sea

Pteria

LYDIA

The Royal Road
Riders carried messages for the Persian king along the 2,500-km Royal Road.

Royal Road

Sardis

Carchemish

SYRIA

Aleppo

Cyprus

felling cedars for shipbuilding

Syrian Desert

beekeeping

Sidon

Tyre

Damascus

Assyrian warfare
The Assyrians were fierce fighters, besieging cities until they surrendered.

Jerusalem

ISRAEL

JUDAH

Babylonian exile
Nebuchadnezzar captured Jerusalem and took all the Jews to Babylon as slaves.

Lake Van • Van

Tigris

Assyrian kings
Kings of Assyria, such as Ashurnasirpal II, had great religious and political power.

Lake Urmia

Assyrian power
The throne room of the king's palace at Nimrud was guarded by two huge stone lions with wings and human faces.

■ NINEVEH
Nimrud
Ashur

Scythian threat
Scythian archers were a constant threat to the Persian armies defending the empire's northern borders.

Caspian Sea

MEDIA

The fatal blow
The Medes joined forces with Babylon to destroy the Assyrian empire in 612BCE.

Hamadan
(Ecbatana)

ASSYRIA

M
E
S
O
P
O
T
A
M
I
A

Euphrates

keeping detailed records on clay tablets

Babylon
Nebuchadnezzar made Babylon the finest city in the world. He built a splendid temple with hanging gardens.

Sippar

BABYLONIA

■ BABYLON

Nippur

Uruk

Ur

Zagros Mountains

SUSA

messenger keeping the king informed about events

Red Sea

Persian Gulf

The great empires

For more than 600 years, three great empires dominated the Middle East. The Assyrians were warlike and brutal, capturing or slaughtering their enemies. Their empire lasted for 300 years until the Babylonians, with the Medes, captured the Assyrian capital of Nineveh in 612BCE. The Babylonians turned Babylon into a fabulous city, but their power was short-lived. In 539BCE the Persians, under Cyrus the Great, seized Babylon and went on to conquer the greatest, most powerful empire the world had ever seen. The Persian kings built beautiful palaces and grew rich on trade and conquest, and their empire lasted for 200 years.

The Persian empire

The Persian kings built magnificent palaces, such as the one at Persepolis, guarded here by rows of stone warriors. From their palaces, the Persian kings ruled such a vast empire that Darius (reigned 521–486BCE) divided it into 20 provinces, called satrapies, each one ruled by an all-powerful ruler called a satrap. To keep the king informed about what his satraps were doing, and other news, a troop of trained riders carried messages along specially built royal roads.

Bactra

Herat

camel trains bringing riches from central Asia

Kandahar

Cyrus the Great
The simple tomb of Cyrus the Great, founder of the Persian empire, still stands at Pasargadae, once the capital of the empire.

Persian soldier
Foot-soldiers in the Persian army covered vast distances during their campaigns.

ELAM

■ PARSAGADAE
■ PERSEPOLIS

P E R S I A

New year palace
The Persian royal palace at Persepolis was occupied only during the new year festivities. The king lived in Susa for the rest of the year.

Zoroastrian fire
In the Zoroastrian religion, fire represents truth, so fires always burned at their altars.

trading ship going to Arabia and India

0	2000	4000 km
0	1000	2000 miles

1000BCE–300BCE

1000BCE

943 Assyrian empire begins to revive under King Ashur-dan II

900BCE

853 Babylonian kings become dependent on Assyrian support

800BCE

729 Assyrians occupy Babylon

700BCE
689 Babylon is sacked after rebelling against Assyrian rule
668–627 Assyrian empire reaches its greatest extent
630–553 Life of Zoroaster, founder of official Persian religion
626 King Nabopolassar of Babylon rebels against Assyrian rule
612 Medes and Babylonians capture Nineveh and destroy Assyrian empire
604–562 Nebuchadnezzar's reign; greatest extent of Babylonian empire

600BCE

559 Cyrus the Great becomes king of Persia and begins to expand his empire
539 Cyrus conquers Babylonian empire
518 Persians conquer Indus Valley in India (outside map area)
513 Persians conquer south-east Europe

500BCE

490–479 Persians try but fail to conquer Greece (outside map area) — this is one of their few setbacks
485 Xerxes, king of Persia, destroys Babylon

400BCE

350 Persian empire dominates Middle East from north Africa to borders of India

300BCE

MACEDON

Mount Olympus
The Greeks believed that their gods and goddesses lived on top of this holy mountain.

Mount Olympus

EPIRUS

Corcyra

Painted pottery
Greek craftsmen produced decorated pots, showing the gods or scenes from their history.

Ambracia

THESSALY

horses were bred in Thessaly

Public speaking
Greek city-states were the first democracies. Politicians spoke to large crowds of citizens.

Thermopylae

AETOLIA

priestess consulting the Oracle at Delphi

BOEOTIA

Delphi

Thebes

ATTICA

Marathon

Athens

Kephallenia

Olympic athletes
The ancient Olympic Games were held once every four years. Winners of each men-only event received a wreath of laurel leaves.

ACHAEA

Sykyon

Megara

Corinth

Argos

Mantinea

Tegea

Olympia

Acropolis
Originally a fort, the Acropolis at Athens was a great complex of shrines and temples dominating the city.

ARCADIA

Sparta

Ancient Greece

Ancient Greece was home to an impressive culture. It was the birthplace of democracy, and many Greek ideas and inventions in philosophy, theatre, architecture, mathematics and medicine still influence us today. Ancient Greece was made up of many independent city-states, which grew up from the 900s BCE. Each had its own laws and way of life. Each city had a market place at its heart, and a fort, or acropolis, built on high ground. City-states were competitive – they fought many wars and, although they formed alliances, they never united to become a country. Athens and Sparta were the most important city-states. Athens was a busy trading city and the first democracy. Sparta was a military state, where all male citizens had to be warriors. Throughout the Greek world, citizens built temples and theatres, where they held festivals involving plays, processions and games.

Warrior state
The city-state of Sparta was known for its tough soldiers, called hoplites.

Mediterranean Sea

Kydonia

CRETE

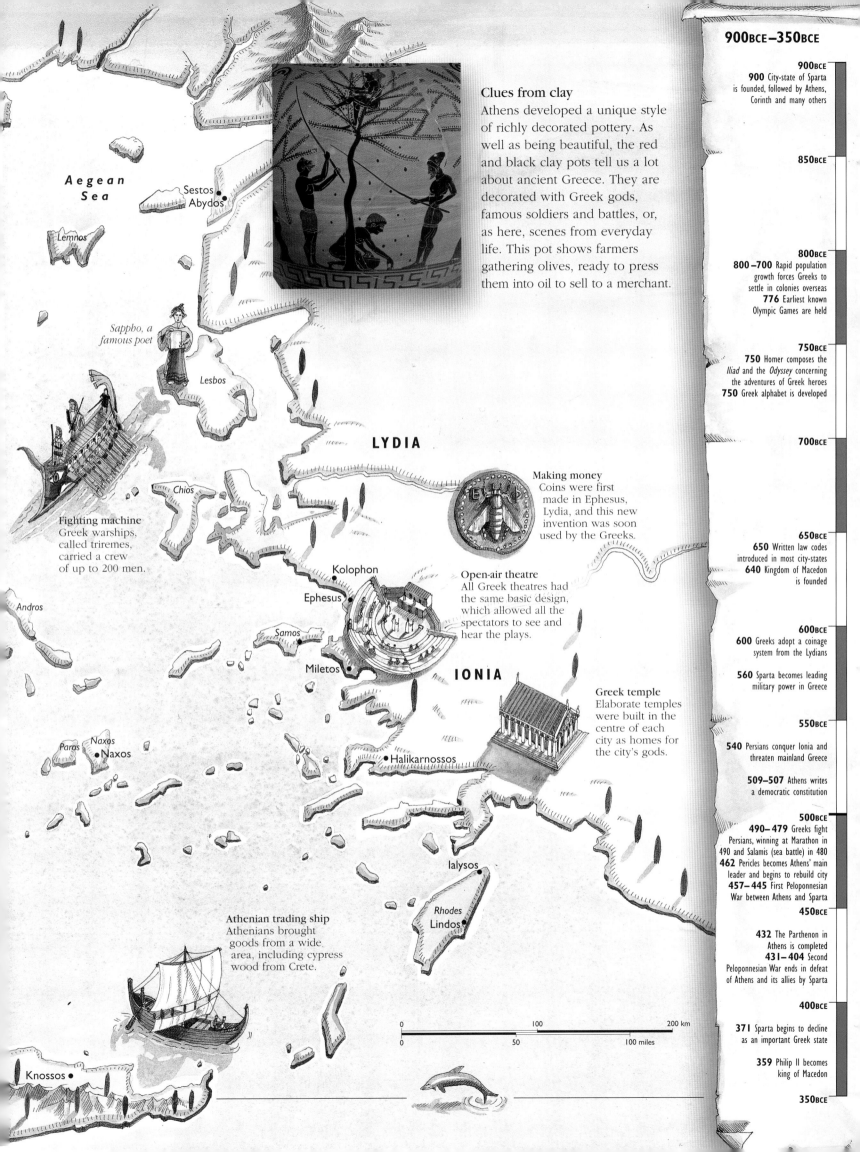

Aegean Sea

Sestos
Abydos

Lemnos

Clues from clay
Athens developed a unique style of richly decorated pottery. As well as being beautiful, the red and black clay pots tell us a lot about ancient Greece. They are decorated with Greek gods, famous soldiers and battles, or, as here, scenes from everyday life. This pot shows farmers gathering olives, ready to press them into oil to sell to a merchant.

Sappho, a famous poet

Lesbos

LYDIA

Chios

Making money
Coins were first made in Ephesus, Lydia, and this new invention was soon used by the Greeks.

Fighting machine
Greek warships, called triremes, carried a crew of up to 200 men.

Andros

Kolophon

Ephesus

Open-air theatre
All Greek theatres had the same basic design, which allowed all the spectators to see and hear the plays.

Samos

Miletos

IONIA

Greek temple
Elaborate temples were built in the centre of each city as homes for the city's gods.

Paros *Naxos*
•**Naxos**

•**Halikarnossos**

Ialysos

Athenian trading ship
Athenians brought goods from a wide area, including cypress wood from Crete.

Rhodes
Lindos

Knossos

0 ——— 100 ——— 200 km
0 —— 50 —— 100 miles

900BCE

900 City-state of Sparta is founded, followed by Athens, Corinth and many others

850BCE

800BCE

800–700 Rapid population growth forces Greeks to settle in colonies overseas
776 Earliest known Olympic Games are held

750BCE

750 Homer composes the *Iliad* and the *Odyssey* concerning the adventures of Greek heroes
750 Greek alphabet is developed

700BCE

650BCE

650 Written law codes introduced in most city-states
640 Kingdom of Macedon is founded

600BCE

600 Greeks adopt a coinage system from the Lydians

560 Sparta becomes leading military power in Greece

550BCE

540 Persians conquer Ionia and threaten mainland Greece

509–507 Athens writes a democratic constitution

500BCE

490–479 Greeks fight Persians, winning at Marathon in 490 and Salamis (sea battle) in 480
462 Pericles becomes Athens' main leader and begins to rebuild city
457–445 First Peloponnesian War between Athens and Sparta

450BCE

432 The Parthenon in Athens is completed
431–404 Second Peloponnesian War ends in defeat of Athens and its allies by Sparta

400BCE

371 Sparta begins to decline as an important Greek state

359 Philip II becomes king of Macedon

350BCE

Ancient Greece:
The Greek World

From around 800BCE, the Greeks founded trading colonies around the shores of the Mediterranean and Black seas. Greece's population had been rising for some time but there was limited fertile land for growing crops to feed everyone. Spreading overseas solved this problem and made the Greeks richer at the same time. Some colonies were very successful, trading iron ore, tin, slaves and wheat in return for wine and other goods. They also spread Greek culture and language throughout a wide region. By the 300s, they had declined in importance as other states, especially Carthage, threatened their livelihood. Greece's fortunes changed, however, in 334, when Alexander the Great invaded the Persian Empire and made Greece the most important nation in the Middle East.

Greek culture

In their many colonies, the Greeks built amphitheatres, such as this one at Miletos in southwest Anatolia (modern-day Turkey), in which to stage plays and hold sporting events. The success of these colonies spread Greek language, literature, law, religion, philosophy, art and architecture far and wide throughout the Mediterranean world, particularly in Sicily and the Etruscan states of northern Italy, and brought great wealth back to Greece itself.

Alexander the Great

Alexander the Great was born in Macedon, northern Greece, in 356BCE. He became king after the death of his father, Philip, in 336, and after a series of epic marches and remarkable victories he conquered the Persian Empire. Although his empire fell apart after his death in 323, it left a lasting legacy of Greek cultural influence, known as Hellenism, that dominated the Mediterranean and the Middle East until the coming of Islam during the 7th century CE. This coin shows Alexander wearing an elephant-scalp headdress to commemorate his victories in India.

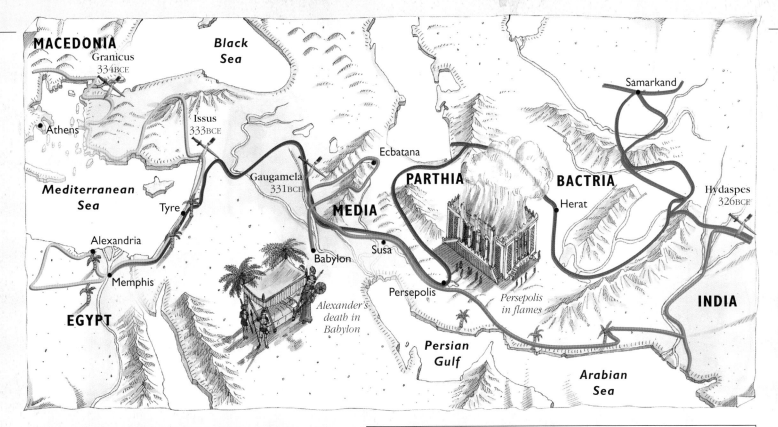

The map shows labels: MACEDONIA, Granicus 334BCE, Black Sea, Athens, Issus 333BCE, Mediterranean Sea, Tyre, Alexandria, Memphis, EGYPT, Gaugamela 331BCE, MEDIA, Babylon, *Alexander's death in Babylon*, Ecbatana, PARTHIA, Susa, Persepolis, *Persepolis in flames*, BACTRIA, Herat, Samarkand, Hydaspes 326BCE, INDIA, Persian Gulf, Arabian Sea

Conquering the world

Alexander and his army crossed into Asia in 334 and defeated a Persian army by the River Granicus. He beat an even larger Persian army at Issus in 333BCE. Having conquered Egypt, he headed into the heart of the Persian Empire, defeating the Persians for the third time at Gaugamela. His march took him into central Asia – destroying the Persian capital, Persepolis, along the way – and on into India, where he achieved his final victory. He died in Babylon in 323, aged only 32.

Alexander's legacy

Alexander left an immense legacy. His empire stretched from Egypt to India and into central Asia, and at least 20 cities bore his name. Alexandria in Egypt soon became one of the greatest cities in the ancient world. It boasted a vast library said to contain all human knowledge of the time. In 2003CE, a vast new library (right) opened in Alexandria to commemorate the ancient library.

KEY TO MAP: lines show four stages in Alexander's march

Battle	334–331BCE
	331–329BCE
	329–326BCE
	326–323BCE

Alexander the Conqueror

Alexander was a superb military commander, leading his Macedon troops into battle often against overwhelming Persian strength. At the Battle of Issus in November 333, Alexander, seen here on horseback on the left of this mosaic, came face to face with the Persian emperor Darius, riding in a war chariot. After his army was defeated, Darius was forced to flee the battlefield, leaving behind most of his family and a vast amount of treasures.

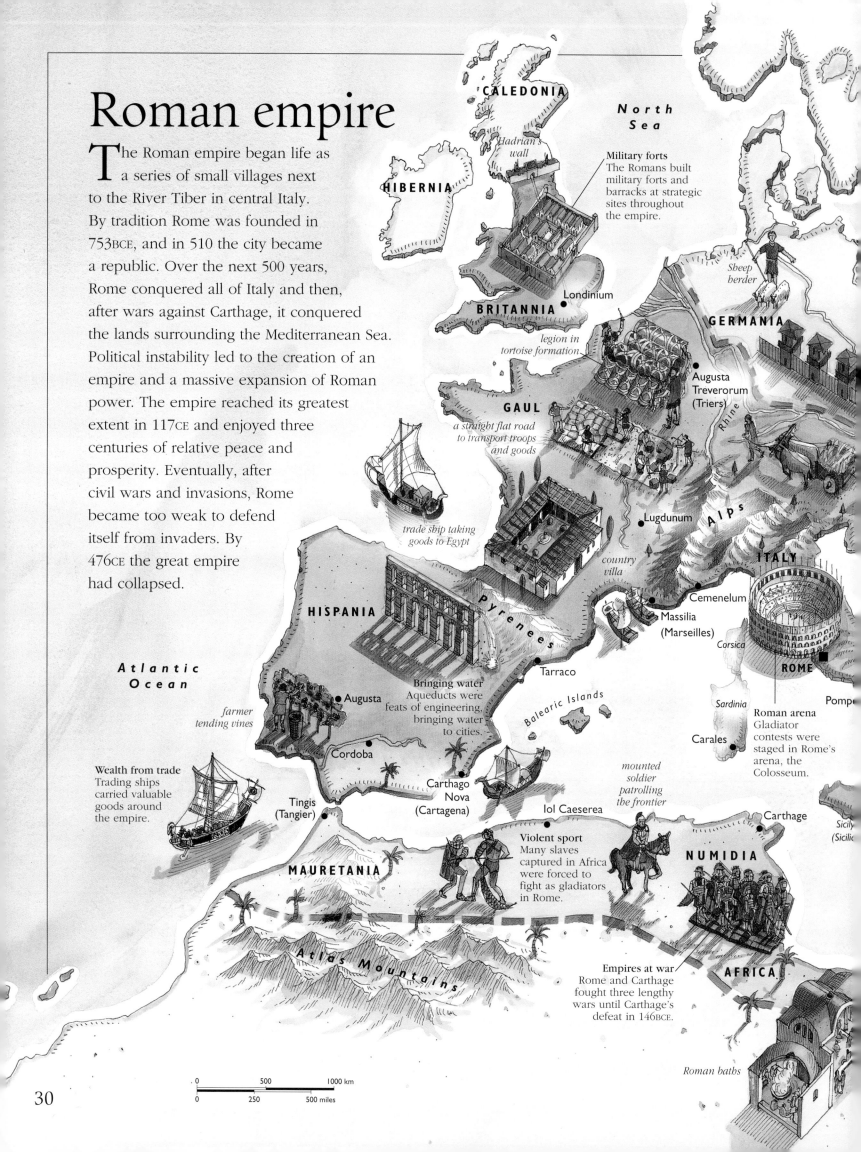

Roman empire

The Roman empire began life as a series of small villages next to the River Tiber in central Italy. By tradition Rome was founded in 753BCE, and in 510 the city became a republic. Over the next 500 years, Rome conquered all of Italy and then, after wars against Carthage, it conquered the lands surrounding the Mediterranean Sea. Political instability led to the creation of an empire and a massive expansion of Roman power. The empire reached its greatest extent in 117CE and enjoyed three centuries of relative peace and prosperity. Eventually, after civil wars and invasions, Rome became too weak to defend itself from invaders. By 476CE the great empire had collapsed.

Military forts
The Romans built military forts and barracks at strategic sites throughout the empire.

Sheep herder

legion in tortoise formation

a straight flat road to transport troops and goods

trade ship taking goods to Egypt

country villa

Bringing water
Aqueducts were feats of engineering, bringing water to cities.

farmer tending vines

Wealth from trade
Trading ships carried valuable goods around the empire.

Roman arena
Gladiator contests were staged in Rome's arena, the Colosseum.

mounted soldier patrolling the frontier

Violent sport
Many slaves captured in Africa were forced to fight as gladiators in Rome.

Empires at war
Rome and Carthage fought three lengthy wars until Carthage's defeat in 146BCE.

Roman baths

CALEDONIA
North Sea
Hadrian's wall
HIBERNIA
BRITANNIA
Londinium
GERMANIA
GAUL
Augusta Treverorum (Triers)
Rhine
Lugdunum
Alps
ITALY
Cemenelum
Massilia (Marseilles)
HISPANIA
Pyrenees
Corsica
ROME
Pomp[e]
Tarraco
Balearic Islands
Sardinia
Atlantic Ocean
Augusta
Carales
Cordoba
Carthago Nova (Cartagena)
Tingis (Tangier)
Iol Caeserea
Carthage
Sicily (Sicili[a])
MAURETANIA
NUMIDIA
Atlas Mountains
AFRICA

0   500   1000 km
0   250   500 miles

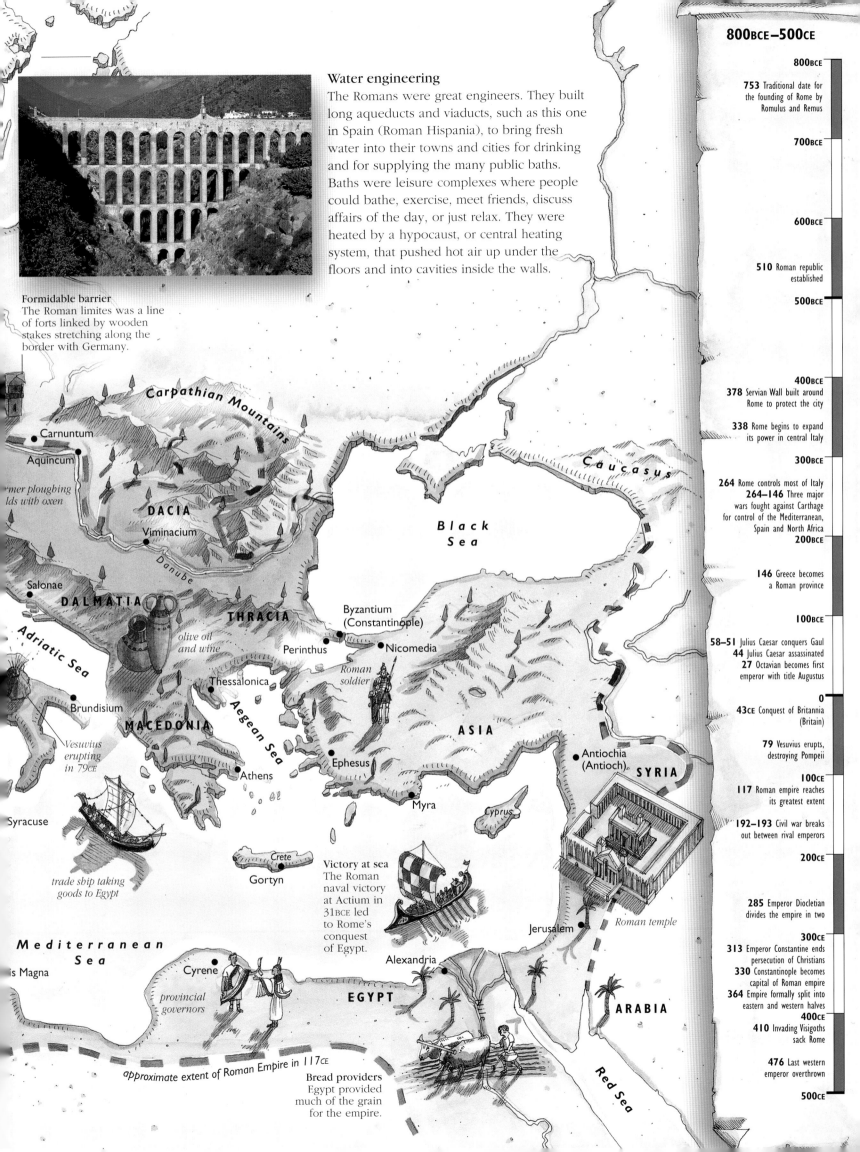

Water engineering

The Romans were great engineers. They built long aqueducts and viaducts, such as this one in Spain (Roman Hispania), to bring fresh water into their towns and cities for drinking and for supplying the many public baths. Baths were leisure complexes where people could bathe, exercise, meet friends, discuss affairs of the day, or just relax. They were heated by a hypocaust, or central heating system, that pushed hot air up under the floors and into cavities inside the walls.

Formidable barrier
The Roman limites was a line of forts linked by wooden stakes stretching along the border with Germany.

mer ploughing lds with oxen

Carpathian Mountains

Carnuntum

Aquincum

DACIA

Viminacium

Danube

Salonae

DALMATIA

olive oil and wine

THRACIA

Black Sea

Caucasus

Byzantium (Constantinople)

Perinthus

Nicomedia

Thessalonica

Roman soldier

ASIA

Antiochia (Antioch)

SYRIA

Adriatic Sea

Brundisium

Vesuvius erupting in 79CE

MACEDONIA

Aegean Sea

Ephesus

Athens

Myra

Cyprus

Roman temple

Syracuse

trade ship taking goods to Egypt

Crete

Gortyn

Victory at sea
The Roman naval victory at Actium in 31BCE led to Rome's conquest of Egypt.

Jerusalem

ARABIA

Mediterranean Sea

s Magna

Cyrene

provincial governors

Alexandria

EGYPT

Red Sea

approximate extent of Roman Empire in 117CE

Bread providers
Egypt provided much of the grain for the empire.

800BCE–500CE

800BCE

753 Traditional date for the founding of Rome by Romulus and Remus

700BCE

600BCE

510 Roman republic established

500BCE

400BCE

378 Servian Wall built around Rome to protect the city

338 Rome begins to expand its power in central Italy

300BCE

264 Rome controls most of Italy
264–146 Three major wars fought against Carthage for control of the Mediterranean, Spain and North Africa

200BCE

146 Greece becomes a Roman province

100BCE

58–51 Julius Caesar conquers Gaul
44 Julius Caesar assassinated
27 Octavian becomes first emperor with title Augustus

0

43CE Conquest of Britannia (Britain)

79 Vesuvius erupts, destroying Pompeii

100CE

117 Roman empire reaches its greatest extent

192–193 Civil war breaks out between rival emperors

200CE

285 Emperor Diocletian divides the empire in two

300CE

313 Emperor Constantine ends persecution of Christians
330 Constantinople becomes capital of Roman empire
364 Empire formally split into eastern and western halves

400CE

410 Invading Visigoths sack Rome

476 Last western emperor overthrown

500CE

Roman empire:
The city of Rome

The imperial city of Rome, capital of the Roman empire, was by far the grandest and most important city in Europe. It was a vast but often shabby city. The first emperor, Augustus (ruled 27BCE–14CE), decided to make it beautiful, too, clearing away narrow streets and building public baths, theatres and temples. He set up a police and fire service to keep its citizens safe, and dredged and widened the River Tiber to prevent its frequent floods. By the end of the 1st century CE, Rome was a showcase for its empire, designed to impress visitors and enemies with the might of the Roman Empire.

Ruling the empire

From 27BCE to 476CE, Rome was governed by emperors. Some, such as Augustus, were outstanding, while others were brutal dictators or madmen. Beneath the emperor was the Senate, an unelected group of about 600 rich men called senators (below), who passed laws, controlled the treasury, and appointed governors to those Roman provinces not run by the emperor himself.

Street life

The streets of Rome were packed with shops selling every type of produce. Bread was made on shop premises (above), while traders brought in fresh food and other goods from outside the city on handcarts, and stocked up their shops each night ready for sale next day. Every street had its local bar, where wine and other drinks were sold, as well as many workshops, where everything from furniture and pots to fine clothes and jewellery were made. Although the main streets were swept clean, most of the smaller ones were very dirty, as people threw their rubbish out of their windows. At night, the city was pitch dark, for there was no street lighting.

Women were separated from men and watched events from their own terrace at the top of the building

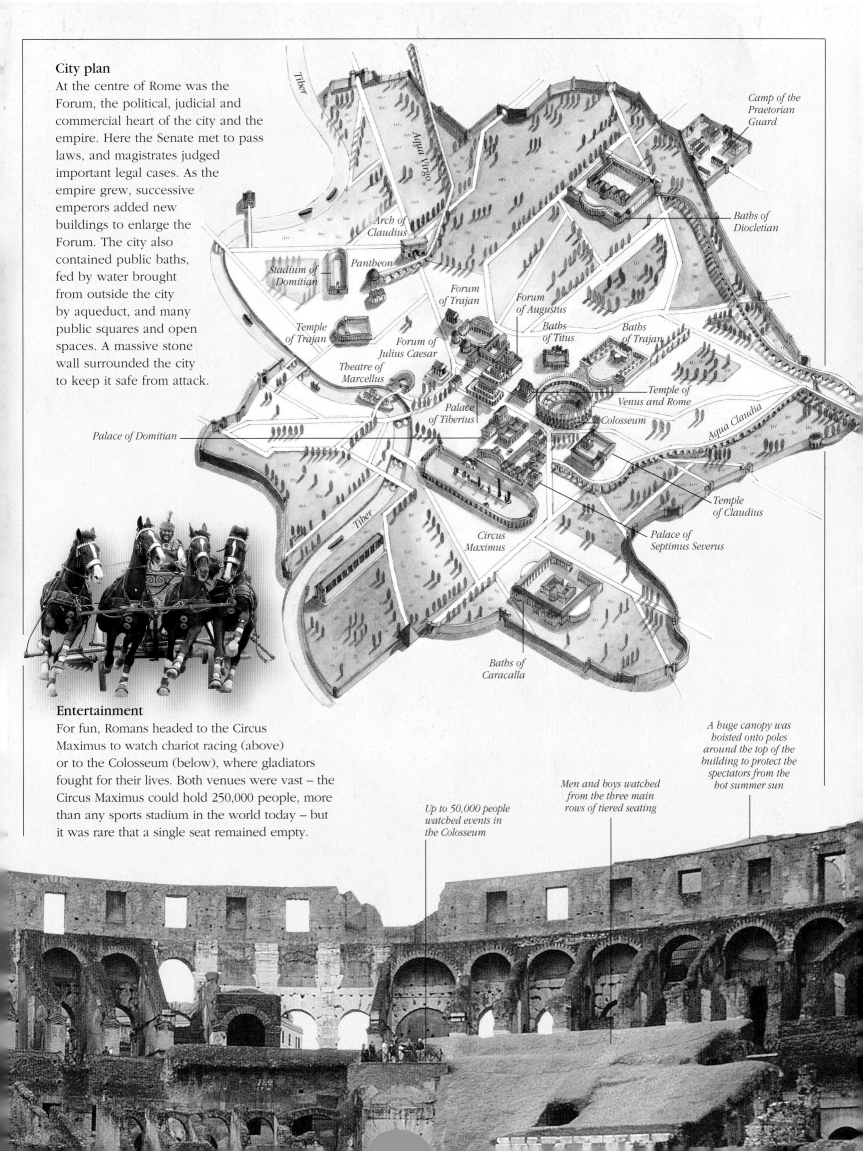

City plan

At the centre of Rome was the Forum, the political, judicial and commercial heart of the city and the empire. Here the Senate met to pass laws, and magistrates judged important legal cases. As the empire grew, successive emperors added new buildings to enlarge the Forum. The city also contained public baths, fed by water brought from outside the city by aqueduct, and many public squares and open spaces. A massive stone wall surrounded the city to keep it safe from attack.

Tiber

Aqua Virgo

Camp of the Praetorian Guard

Baths of Diocletian

Arch of Claudius

Pantheon

Stadium of Domitian

Forum of Trajan

Forum of Augustus

Baths of Titus

Baths of Trajan

Temple of Trajan

Forum of Julius Caesar

Theatre of Marcellus

Palace of Tiberius

Temple of Venus and Rome

Colosseum

Palace of Domitian

Aqua Claudia

Temple of Claudius

Palace of Septimus Severus

Tiber

Circus Maximus

Baths of Caracalla

Entertainment

For fun, Romans headed to the Circus Maximus to watch chariot racing (above) or to the Colosseum (below), where gladiators fought for their lives. Both venues were vast – the Circus Maximus could hold 250,000 people, more than any sports stadium in the world today – but it was rare that a single seat remained empty.

A huge canopy was hoisted onto poles around the top of the building to protect the spectators from the hot summer sun

Men and boys watched from the three main rows of tiered seating

Up to 50,000 people watched events in the Colosseum

Ancient Africa

About 5,500 years ago, the grassy plains of the Sahara began to dry out and turn to desert, cutting Africa in half. Until the introduction of the camel from Arabia in about 100BCE, there was little communication across this sandy desert. Many great civilizations flourished south of the Sahara. The oldest of these was in Nubia on the upper reaches of the Nile. At one time the Nubian kingdom was so powerful it ruled all of Egypt, but its successor Meroë was eventually conquered by the Christian kingdom of Axum, forerunner of modern-day Ethiopia. In the west, the people of Nok learned to work iron, and produced beautiful terracotta figures. The neighbouring Bantus were also skilled ironworkers, gradually spreading their language and technology east and south to all but the very southern tip of Africa. In many places, however, Africans remained in the Stone Age, hunting and gathering their food from the forests and plains around them.

Rock art
Farmers painted pictures on rocks in the once-fertile Sahara as long ago as 6000BCE.

date palms

camels helping trade across the Sahara

Gold mining
Gold was mined in the forests of west Africa and made into official regalia and jewellery.

Atlantic Ocean

Nok culture
From about 500BCE, Nok craftworkers produced beautiful terracotta heads and figures, among the earliest surviving artworks from Africa south of the Sahara. They also learned to smelt iron ore to produce weapons and tools, a valuable skill when most of their enemies had only wooden spears and stones to use against them. Further up the Niger river valley, the city of Jenne-jeno, the earliest-known town in sub-Saharan Africa, became the hub of trade across the Sahara, where traders used camels to carry gold, silver, ivory and salt across the desert.

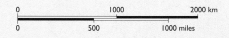

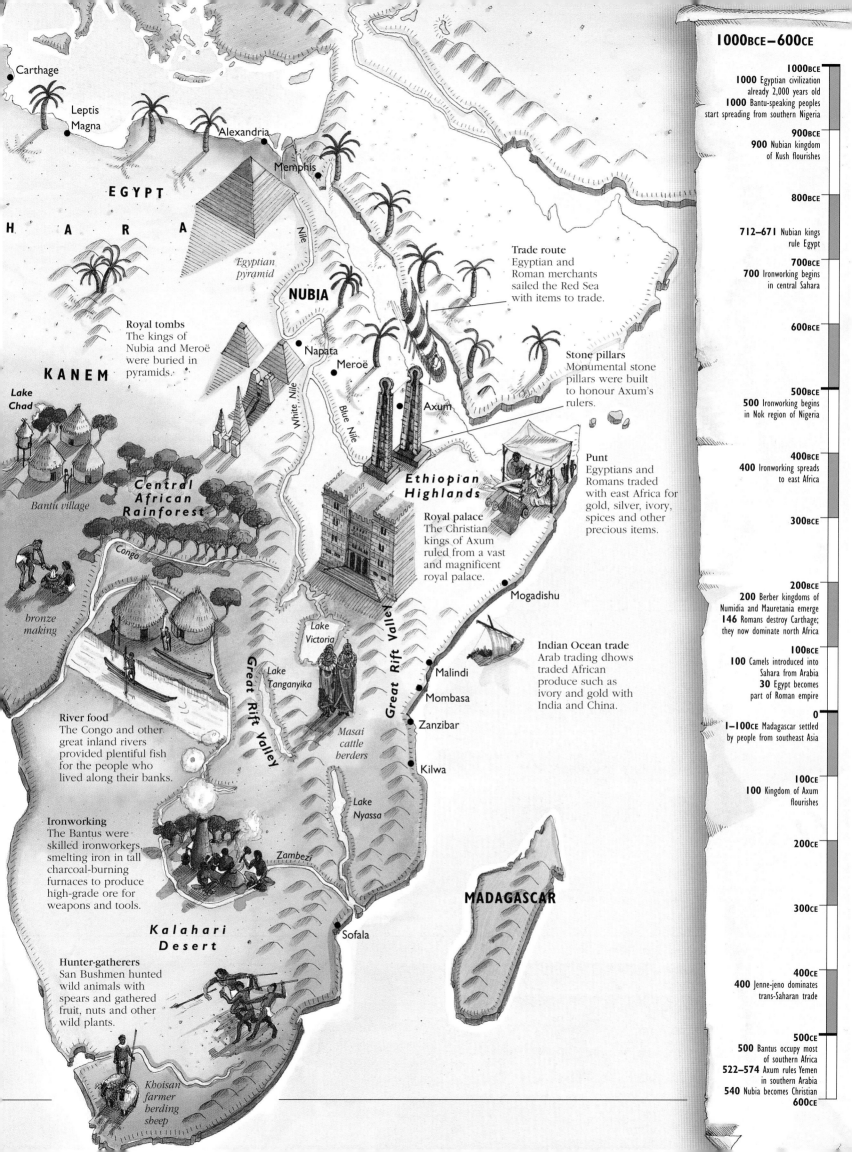

Carthage

Leptis
Magna

Alexandria

EGYPT

Memphis

Nile

Egyptian pyramid

S A H A R A

NUBIA

Royal tombs
The kings of
Nubia and Meroë
were buried in
pyramids.

Napata

Meroë

White Nile

Blue Nile

Axum

KANEM

Lake
Chad

Bantu village

**Central
African
Rainforest**

Congo

*bronze
making*

**Ethiopian
Highlands**

Stone pillars
Monumental stone
pillars were built
to honour Axum's
rulers.

Trade route
Egyptian and
Roman merchants
sailed the Red Sea
with items to trade.

Punt
Egyptians and
Romans traded
with east Africa for
gold, silver, ivory,
spices and other
precious items.

Royal palace
The Christian
kings of Axum
ruled from a vast
and magnificent
royal palace.

Mogadishu

River food
The Congo and other
great inland rivers
provided plentiful fish
for the people who
lived along their banks.

Lake
Victoria

Great Rift Valley

Lake
Tanganyika

*Masai
cattle
herders*

Great Rift Valley

Malindi

Mombasa

Zanzibar

Indian Ocean trade
Arab trading dhows
traded African
produce such as
ivory and gold with
India and China.

Kilwa

Ironworking
The Bantus were
skilled ironworkers,
smelting iron in tall
charcoal-burning
furnaces to produce
high-grade ore for
weapons and tools.

Zambezi

Lake
Nyassa

MADAGASCAR

**Kalahari
Desert**

Sofala

Hunter-gatherers
San Bushmen hunted
wild animals with
spears and gathered
fruit, nuts and other
wild plants.

*Khoisan
farmer
herding
sheep*

1000BCE–600CE

1000BCE

1000 Egyptian civilization
already 2,000 years old
1000 Bantu-speaking peoples
start spreading from southern Nigeria

900BCE

900 Nubian kingdom
of Kush flourishes

800BCE

712–671 Nubian kings
rule Egypt

700BCE

700 Ironworking begins
in central Sahara

600BCE

500BCE

500 Ironworking begins
in Nok region of Nigeria

400BCE

400 Ironworking spreads
to east Africa

300BCE

200BCE

200 Berber kingdoms of
Numidia and Mauretania emerge
146 Romans destroy Carthage;
they now dominate north Africa

100BCE

100 Camels introduced into
Sahara from Arabia
30 Egypt becomes
part of Roman empire

0

1–100CE Madagascar settled
by people from southeast Asia

100CE

100 Kingdom of Axum
flourishes

200CE

300CE

400CE

400 Jenne-jeno dominates
trans-Saharan trade

500CE

500 Bantus occupy most
of southern Africa
522–574 Axum rules Yemen
in southern Arabia
540 Nubia becomes Christian

600CE

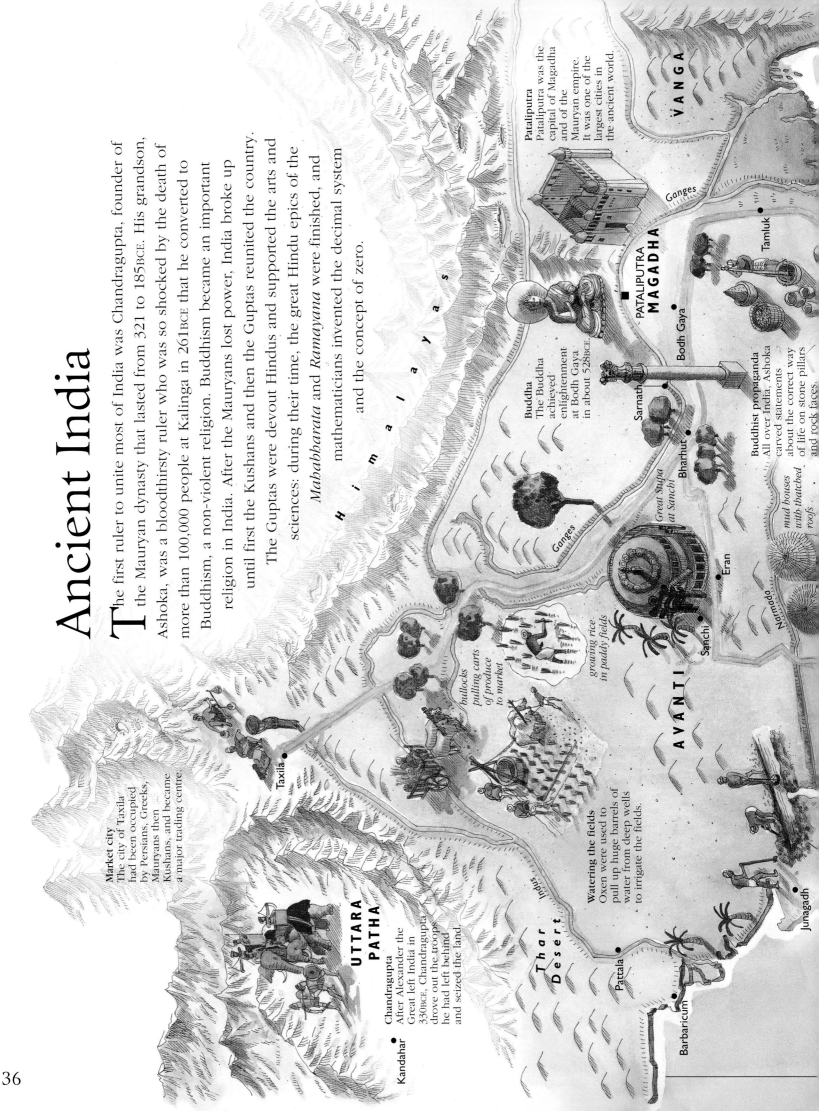

Ancient India

The first ruler to unite most of India was Chandragupta, founder of the Mauryan dynasty that lasted from 321 to 185BCE. His grandson, Ashoka, was a bloodthirsty ruler who was so shocked by the death of more than 100,000 people at Kalinga in 261BCE that he converted to Buddhism, a non-violent religion. Buddhism became an important religion in India. After the Mauryans lost power, India broke up until first the Kushans and then the Guptas reunited the country.

The Guptas were devout Hindus and supported the arts and sciences: during their time, the great Hindu epics of the *Mahabharata* and *Ramayana* were finished, and mathematicians invented the decimal system and the concept of zero.

Himalayas

Patliputra
Patliputra was the capital of Magadha and of the Mauryan empire. It was one of the largest cities in the ancient world.

Ganges

V A N G A

• Tamluk

PATALIPUTRA
MAGADHA

• Bodh Gaya

Buddha
The Buddha achieved enlightenment at Bodh Gaya in about 528BCE.

• Sarnath

Buddhist propaganda
All over India, Ashoka carved statements about the correct way of life on stone pillars and rock faces.

Great Stupa at Sanchi

• Bharhut

mud houses with thatched roofs

• Eran

Ganges

• Sanchi

Narmada

growing rice in paddy fields

A V A N T I

bullocks pulling carts of produce to market

Market city
The city of Taxila had been occupied by Persians, Greeks, Mauryans then Kushans, and became a major trading centre.

• Taxila

Watering the fields
Oxen were used to pull up huge barrels of water from deep wells to irrigate the fields.

Indus

T h a r   D e s e r t

• Pattala

U T T A R A   P A T H A

Chandragupta
After Alexander the Great left India in 330BCE, Chandragupta drove out the troops he had left behind and seized the land.

• Kandahar

• Barbaricum

• Junagadh

36

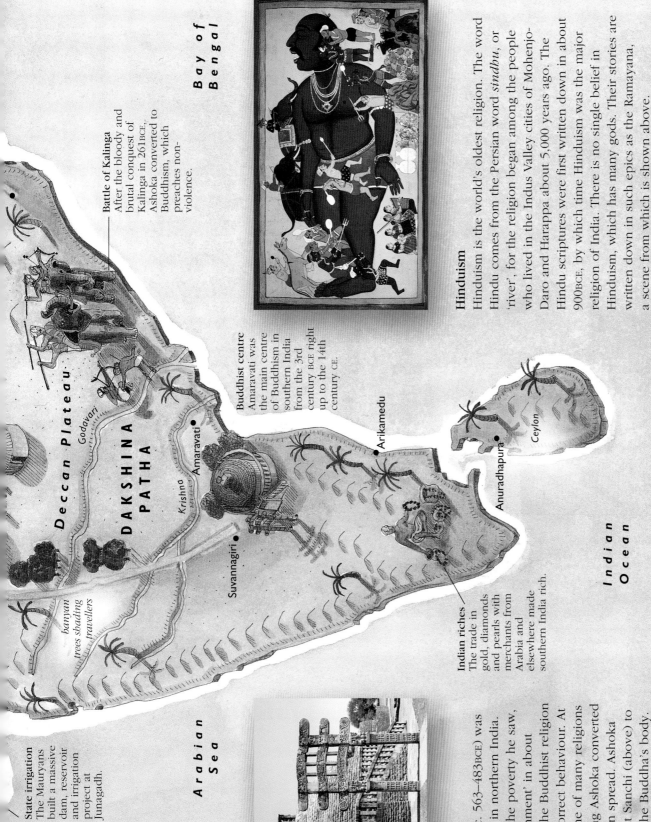

Battle of Kalinga
After the bloody and brutal conquest of Kalinga in 261BCE, Ashoka converted to Buddhism, which preaches non-violence.

Buddhist centre
Amaravati was the main centre of Buddhism in southern India from the 3rd century BCE right up to the 14th century CE.

Indian riches
The trade in gold, diamonds and pearls with merchants from Arabia and elsewhere made southern India rich.

State irrigation
The Mauryans built a massive dam, reservoir and irrigation project at Junagadh.

banyan trees shading travellers

Bay of Bengal

Deccan Plateau

Godavari

DAKSHINA PATHA

Krishna

● Amaravati

● Arikamedu

● Suvannagiri

Ceylon

● Anuradhapura

Indian Ocean

Arabian Sea

Hinduism

Hinduism is the world's oldest religion. The word Hindu comes from the Persian word *sindhu*, or 'river', for the religion began among the people who lived in the Indus Valley cities of Mohenjo-Daro and Harappa about 5,000 years ago. The Hindu scriptures were first written down in about 900BCE, by which time Hinduism was the major religion of India. There is no single belief in Hinduism, which has many gods. Their stories are written down in such epics as the Ramayana, a scene from which is shown above.

Buddhism

Siddhartha Gautama (c. 563–483BCE) was born a wealthy prince in northern India. He was distressed by the poverty he saw, and after his 'enlightenment' in about 528BCE he developed the Buddhist religion of non-violence and correct behaviour. At first, Buddhism was one of many religions in India, but when King Ashoka converted to it in 260, the religion spread. Ashoka built the Great Stupa at Sanchi (above) to house the remains of the Buddha's body.

0   200   400 miles

0   400   800 km

500BCE
500 Magadha is the main Hindu kingdom in northern India
500 The *Mahabharata* is first written down
483 Vijaya founds first kingdom in Ceylon
483 Death of Buddha

400BCE
364 Under the Nanda dynasty, Magadha dominates the Ganges Valley
327–325 Alexander the Great conquers Indus Valley
321 Chandragupta Maurya seizes power in Magadha

300BCE
300 The *Ramayana* is written down
293 Chandragupta Maurya abdicates in favour of Bindusara Maurya, who conquers southern India
268–233 Ashoka rules Mauryan empire

200BCE
185 Mauryan empire overthrown

100BCE

0

50CE Kushans conquer northwest India

100CE
130 Kushan empire at its peak

200CE
200 Hindu laws are first written down

300CE
320–335 Chandragupta I, founder of Mauryan dynasty, rules
335–380 Samudragupta conquers Kushan empire
380 Chandragupta II conquers western India
400CE

500CE
510 Gupta empire begins to decline, finally ending in 720

575 Indian mathematicians develop decimal system and concept of zero

600CE

Ancient China

In 221 BCE, Zheng, ruler of Qin in central China, defeated his rivals and united China. He took the title Qin Shi Huangdi, or 'first sovereign Qin emperor'. Ever since 1122 BCE, China had in theory been united under the Zhou kings, but real power lay with the many provincial leaders, who often had more power than the king himself. Shi Huangdi changed all this by setting up a strong state where all power rested with the emperor. He built the Great Wall to keep out invaders, as well as many roads and canals, but after his death a civil war broke out and the Han dynasty of rulers came to power in 202 BCE. The Han expanded the empire south and east, but when they were overthrown in 220 CE, China split into three kingdoms.

The Great Wall
The first emperor joined various state and city walls to form a single barrier 3,460km across the north of China. It was built of rammed earth reinforced with brushwood.

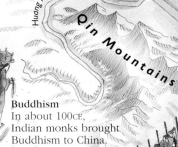

Dunhuang

The Silk Road
Merchants used camels to carry silk and other valuable goods along the Silk Road, which connected China to western Asia and Europe.

Huang He (Yellow River)

Qin Mountains

Silk Road

Qin

Buddhism
In about 100 CE, Indian monks brought Buddhism to China.

tea growing in hilly areas

Terracotta army
When Qin Shi Huangdi died, he was buried with 7,000 lifelike terracotta soldiers, to guard him in the afterlife.

Buddhism

The Buddhist religion was introduced to China by monks from India – one of whom is shown here with Buddha himself – around 100 CE. The peaceful teachings of Buddhism appealed to the Chinese during the troubled years after the fall of the Han dynasty in 220 CE, and it soon became one of China's three major religions, alongside Confucianism and Daoism. The monks travelled into China along the Silk Road, a series of trade routes that connected the major cities of China with central Asia, the eastern Mediterranean and eventually Rome. Merchants travelled the road carrying silk, jade and, much later, fine porcelain.

Jiaozhi

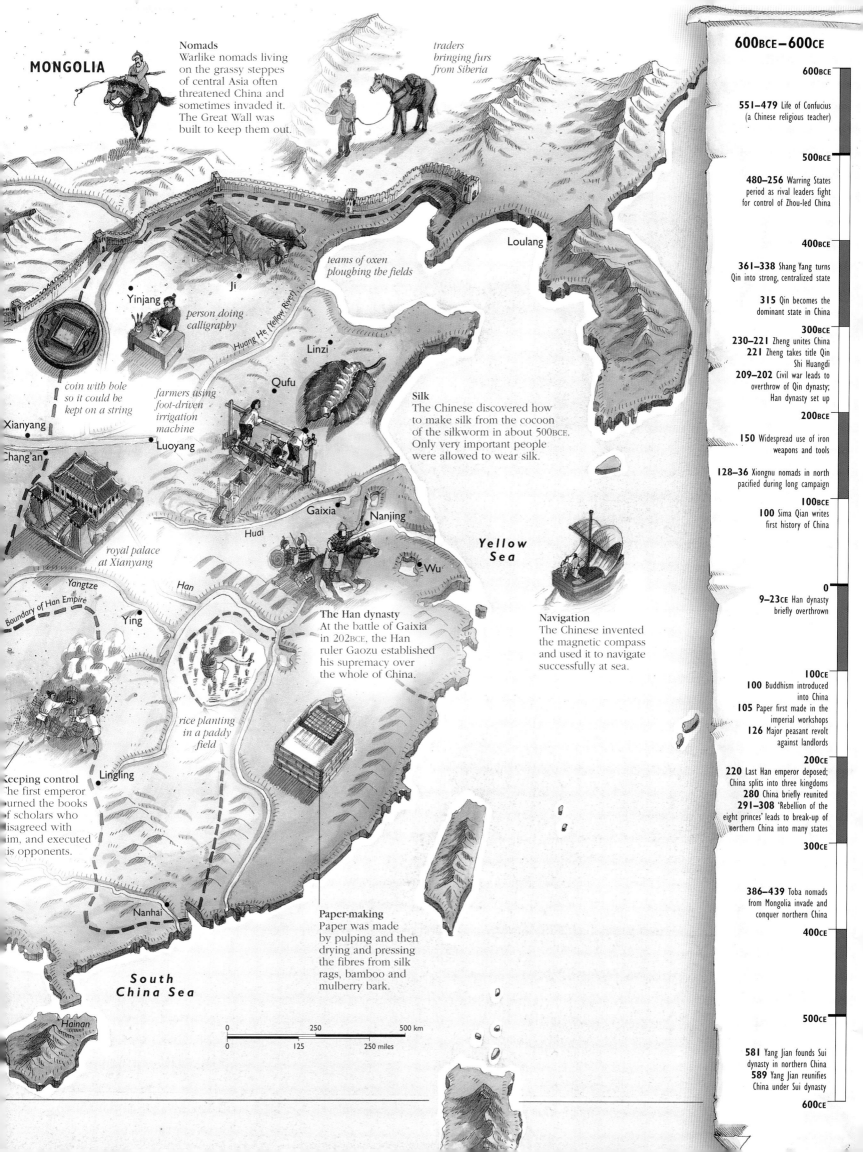

MONGOLIA

Nomads
Warlike nomads living on the grassy steppes of central Asia often threatened China and sometimes invaded it. The Great Wall was built to keep them out.

traders bringing furs from Siberia

Loulang

teams of oxen ploughing the fields

Ji

Yinjang

person doing calligraphy

Huang He (Yellow River)

Linzi

Qufu

coin with hole so it could be kept on a string

farmers using foot-driven irrigation machine

Xianyang

Chang'an

Luoyang

Silk
The Chinese discovered how to make silk from the cocoon of the silkworm in about 500BCE. Only very important people were allowed to wear silk.

Gaixia

Nanjing

Huai

royal palace at Xianyang

Yellow Sea

Wu

Yangtze

Boundary of Han Empire

Han

Ying

The Han dynasty
At the battle of Gaixia in 202BCE, the Han ruler Gaozu established his supremacy over the whole of China.

Navigation
The Chinese invented the magnetic compass and used it to navigate successfully at sea.

rice planting in a paddy field

Keeping control
The first emperor burned the books of scholars who disagreed with him, and executed his opponents.

Lingling

Paper-making
Paper was made by pulping and then drying and pressing the fibres from silk rags, bamboo and mulberry bark.

Nanhai

South China Sea

Hainan

0   250   500 km

0   125   250 miles

600BCE–600CE

600BCE

551–479 Life of Confucius (a Chinese religious teacher)

500BCE

480–256 Warring States period as rival leaders fight for control of Zhou-led China

400BCE

361–338 Shang Yang turns Qin into strong, centralized state

315 Qin becomes the dominant state in China

300BCE

230–221 Zheng unites China
221 Zheng takes title Qin Shi Huangdi
209–202 Civil war leads to overthrow of Qin dynasty; Han dynasty set up

200BCE

150 Widespread use of iron weapons and tools

128–36 Xiongnu nomads in north pacified during long campaign

100BCE

100 Sima Qian writes first history of China

0

9–23CE Han dynasty briefly overthrown

100CE

100 Buddhism introduced into China
105 Paper first made in the imperial workshops
126 Major peasant revolt against landlords

200CE

220 Last Han emperor deposed; China splits into three kingdoms
280 China briefly reunited
291–308 'Rebellion of the eight princes' leads to break-up of northern China into many states

300CE

386–439 Toba nomads from Mongolia invade and conquer northern China

400CE

500CE

581 Yang Jian founds Sui dynasty in northern China
589 Yang Jian reunifies China under Sui dynasty

600CE

North American peoples

The first people arrived in North America from Siberia over the land bridge that existed about 17,000 years ago. They slowly moved southwards, spreading out over the vast plains, woodlands, deserts and mountains of the continent, living as hunter-gatherers as they went. From about 700BCE, the Adena people of the Ohio river valley began to cultivate wild plants for food, and built sacred earthworks and burial mounds. The later Hopewell people, who spread out from the Ohio into the Mississippi Valley, built towns, burial mounds, and a huge earthwork in the shape of a snake, although no one really knows why they did this. The people of the southwestern deserts began to settle down in farming communities by about 300CE, eventually building complex villages of adobe (dried mud) brick houses. In the far north of America, the Inuit learned how to live in the cold conditions, trapping wild animals for their fur, meat and bone.

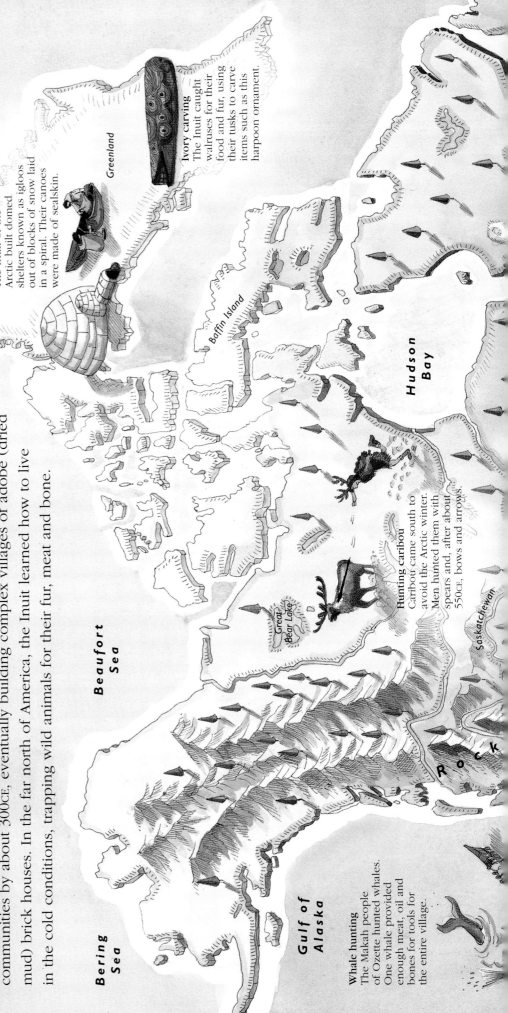

The Inuit
The Inuit of the Arctic built domed shelters known as igloos out of blocks of snow laid in a spiral. Their canoes were made of sealskin.

Greenland

Ivory carving
The Inuit caught walruses for their food and fur, using their tusks to carve items such as this harpoon ornament.

Greenland Sea

Baffin Island

Hudson Bay

Beaufort Sea

Great Bear Lake

Hunting caribou
Caribou came south to avoid the Arctic winter. Men hunted them with spears and, after about 550CE, bows and arrows.

Saskatchewan

Rock

Bering Sea

Gulf of Alaska

Whale hunting
The Makah people of Ozette hunted whales. One whale provided enough meat, oil and bones for tools for the entire village.

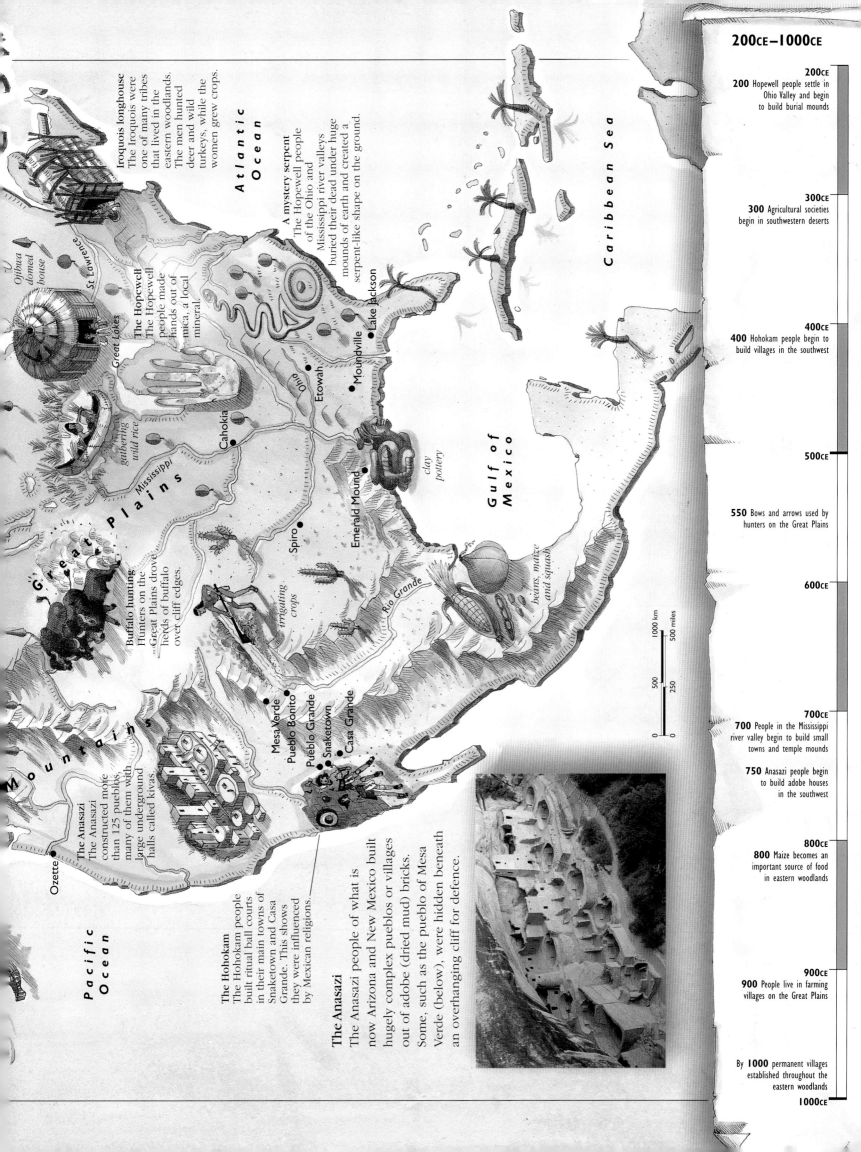

Map labels and text

Iroquois longhouse
The Iroquois were one of many tribes that lived in the eastern woodlands. The men hunted deer and wild turkeys, while the women grew crops.

Atlantic Ocean

Ojibwa domed house

A mystery serpent
The Hopewell people of the Ohio and Mississippi river valleys buried their dead under huge mounds of earth and created a serpent-like shape on the ground.

St Lawrence

Great Lakes

The Hopewell
The Hopewell people made hands out of mica, a local mineral.

gathering wild rice

Caribbean Sea

Lake Jackson

Ohio

Etowah
Moundville

Mississippi

Cahokia

Great Plains

Buffalo hunting
Hunters on the Great Plains drove herds of buffalo over cliff edges.

clay pottery

Gulf of Mexico

Emerald Mound

Spiro

irrigating crops

Rio Grande

beans, maize and squash

Mountains

Mesa Verde
Pueblo Bonito
Pueblo Grande
Snaketown
Casa Grande

The Hohokam
The Hohokam people built ritual ball courts in their main towns of Snaketown and Casa Grande. This shows they were influenced by Mexican religions.

Ozette

The Anasazi
The Anasazi constructed more than 125 pueblos, many of them with large underground halls called kivas.

Pacific Ocean

The Anasazi
The Anasazi people of what is now Arizona and New Mexico built hugely complex pueblos or villages out of adobe (dried mud) bricks. Some, such as the pueblo of Mesa Verde (below), were hidden beneath an overhanging cliff for defence.

Scale: 1000 km / 500 miles; 500 / 250; 0

200CE
200 Hopewell people settle in Ohio Valley and begin to build burial mounds

300CE
300 Agricultural societies begin in southwestern deserts

400CE
400 Hohokam people begin to build villages in the southwest

500CE

550 Bows and arrows used by hunters on the Great Plains

600CE

700CE
700 People in the Mississippi river valley begin to build small towns and temple mounds

750 Anasazi people begin to build adobe houses in the southwest

800CE
800 Maize becomes an important source of food in eastern woodlands

900CE
900 People live in farming villages on the Great Plains

By **1000** permanent villages established throughout the eastern woodlands

1000CE

Central and South America

A series of ancient civilizations, most based around a single city, rose and fell in Central and South America between 1000BCE and 1000CE. The Olmecs built ceremonial earth pyramid mounds and carved huge stone sculptures. To their north, the city of Teotihuacan grew larger than Rome and contained the biggest building in the ancient Americas: the Pyramid of the Sun. The major civilization in the region was the Maya, who built massive pyramid temple complexes and were skilled mathematicians and astronomers. In South America, Andean people built a huge stone temple mound with rooms filled with stone carvings of their gods. The Moche were skilled pottery makers, while the stonemasons of Tiahuanaco built vast temples and palaces.

Teotihuacan
The city of Teotihuacan started as a small village but grew by 500ce to cover 20km² and house perhaps 200,000 people. At its centre were the vast pyramids of the Sun and Moon.

nose pendant (worn by nobility)

Olmec stone sculpture

Mayan men playing ball game

Mayan temple
The Mayans built their temples on top of stepped pyramids. A new temple was dedicated to the gods by sacrificing prisoners captured during a war.

Mayan writing
The Maya wrote with hieroglyphic picture writing. Each glyph represented a syllable.

Pyramid at Copán
Copán was one of the most important cites in the Mayan empire and flourished during the 600s. The ruler of Copán was buried in this step pyramid which dominates the city.

Gulf of Mexico

Caribbean Sea

Pacific Ocean

Andes

weaving with alpaca and llama wool

Chichén Itzá

Tikal

Copán

Yucatan Peninsula

Palenque

Tres Zapotes

San Lorenzo

Teotihuacan

Monte Albán

jaguar

wild turkey kept for food

jade necklace from Teotihuacan

fishing from a reed boat

SOUTH AMERICA

steep hillsides terraced and irrigated for farming

fishing on Lake Titicaca

Andes

gold panning in Andean streams

Lake Titicaca

Tiahuanaco

Alto Rairez

San Pedro de Atacama

Huarpa

Huari

Nazca

Pampa Ingenio

maize grown in irrigated fields

Moche

Pañamarca

Viracocha

Cerro Vicus Pampa Grande

Moche warrior graves

Moche
Moche, capital of the Moche state, contained two huge adobe (mud-brick) platforms dedicated to the sun and moon and a vast royal burial site.

Tiahuanaco
The highest city in the Andes controlled a large empire. At its heart was a precinct of temples and palaces and the stone Gateway of the Sun.

Nazca Lines
The Nazca people drew huge geometric shapes and outlines of animals, birds and insects in the desert sands.

The Maya

The Maya settled in central America from about 1000BCE. They began to build temple pyramids on which to worship their gods and by 350BCE were creating powerful city-states, such as Palenque, Tikal and Copán. The Mayans created the only complete picture writing system in the ancient Americas. It was a sophisticated system that could fully express their entire spoken language. They were also skilled mathematicians and studied the stars to draw up a detailed calendar that told them when eclipses of the sun and moon occurred.

Maya city-states dominated the region from 300 to 800CE, but then went into decline for reasons no one today fully understands. The exception was the northern city of Chichén Itzá, founded in about 850CE, which was dominated by the Castillo pyramid shown above. Eventually Chichén Itzá itself declined and was overrun by the Toltecs, which brought Mayan civilization to an end.

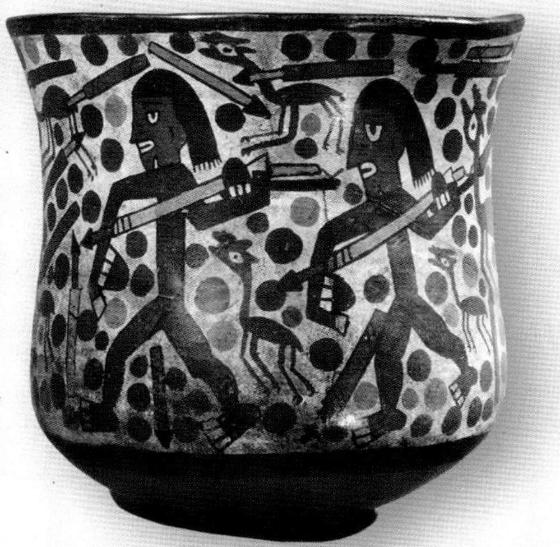

The Nazca

The Nazca people, like many others in South America, were skilled potters, creating this beautiful painted vase showing men hunting vicuna, a llama-like animal. The Nazca lived in the coastal plains of Peru, much of which was hot, dry desert. Here, they scratched into the sand vast outlines of figures, including a spider, a hummingbird and a monkey, and geometric shapes. These shapes are so big that they can only be seen properly from the sky. No one really knows why the Nazca created these shapes.

1000 km

500 miles

500BCE
500 Olmec civilization flourishes by the Gulf of Mexico
450 Monte Alban is centre of Zapotec culture

400BCE
400 Chavin de Huantar culture spreads throughout central Andes
350 First Maya city-state built in Yucatan Peninsula

300BCE
300 Olmec civilization declines

200BCE
200 City of Teotihuacan founded
200 Nazcas begin to draw lines in Peruvian desert
150 Maya first develop their picture writing around this time

100BCE
100 Moche state created in northern Peru

0

100CE
150 Pyramid of the Sun built in Teotihuacan

200CE
200 People in Huarpa begin to terrace and irrigate the Andes for agriculture

300CE
300 Moche state at its most powerful

400CE
450 Tikal is main Maya city-state

500CE
500 Huari state begins to create empire in central Andes

600CE
600 Tiahuanaco empire dominates southern Andes region

700CE
700 Huari empire overruns Moche
700 Teotihuacan sacked by armies from nearby rival city

800CE
800 Maya city-states begin to decline
850 Chichén Itzá, last major Maya city-state, founded

900CE
900 Centre of Mayan civilization moves north to Chichén Itzá
950 Toltecs migrate from Mexico and overrun remaining Maya city-states

1000CE

Australia and Polynesia

Some 40,000 years ago, nomadic people from southeast Asia arrived and settled in Australia. These Aboriginals – the name we give to the original inhabitants of a country – were hunter-gatherers and, apart from in the far north of Australia, remained isolated from the rest of the world until the 18th century CE. The Polynesians gradually settled on the isolated islands of the Pacific Ocean in one of the most extraordinary feats of exploration in human history. With no navigational aids apart from the sun and stars, they sailed their canoes over vast expanses of ocean, observing wind and wave patterns, the formation of clouds, and the flight of birds to locate islands hidden over the horizon. By 1000CE they had reached their final destination – Aotearoa, the islands we call New Zealand.

North Pacific Ocean

Eating well
Polynesians kept chickens, dogs and pigs, grew bananas, breadfruit, sweet potatoes, yams and other crops.

Coral Sea

Gulf of Carpentaria

Living in the sky
Aboriginals living on the swampy northern coastline built huts on raised platforms to guard against snakes.

people telling Dreamtime stories

Great Sandy Desert

grinding grass seeds between stones for food

Uluru
This vast rock has always been a sacred place for aboriginals. Here and at other sacred sites, they would perform dances, accompanied by a didgeridoo.

Uluru

AUSTRALIA

hunting for turtles using outrigger canoes

Great Dividing Range

Kangaroo hunting
Aboriginals hunted kangaroos for their meat with spears and boomerangs, curved sticks that returned when thrown.

searching for edible roots

digging a well for water

fishing with nets in eastern rivers

Darling

Lachlan

Murray

Great Australian Bight

Tasman Sea

collecting seashells to trade for other items

Tasmania

0   1000   2000 km
0   500   1000 miles

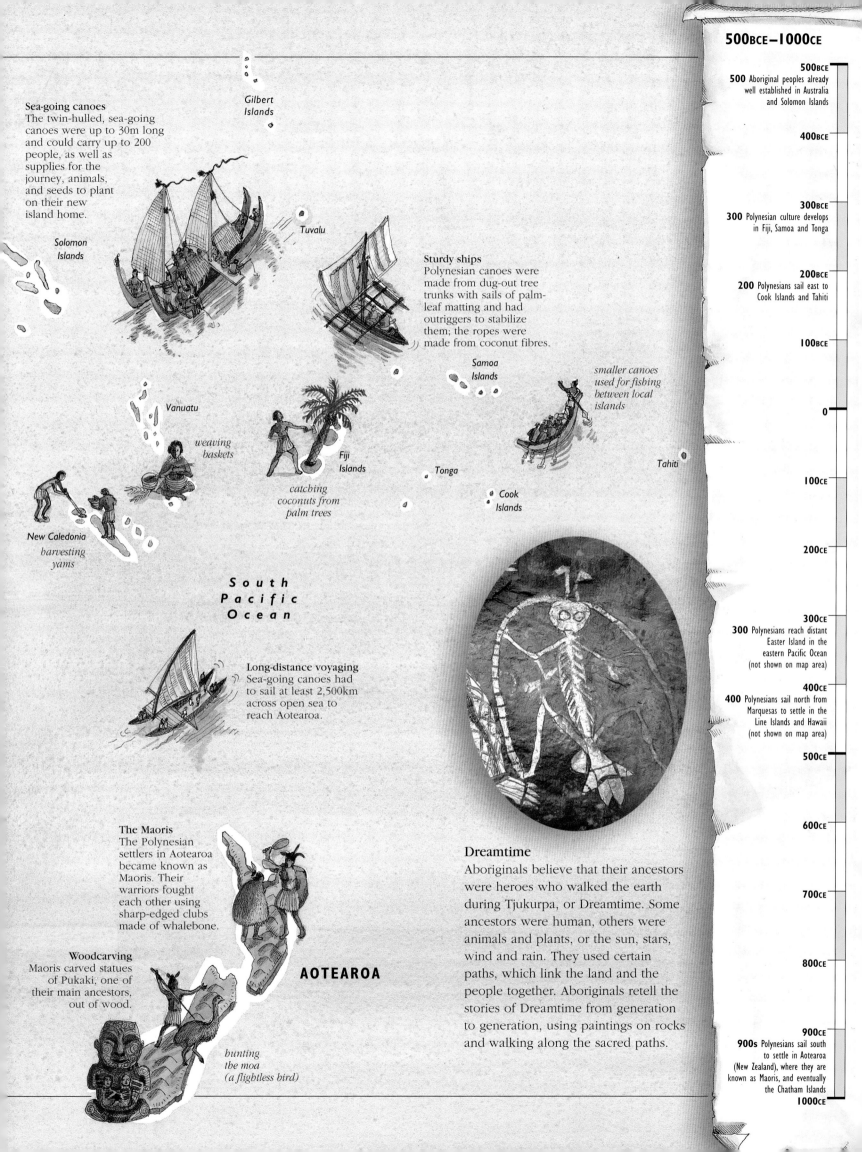

Sea-going canoes
The twin-hulled, sea-going canoes were up to 30m long and could carry up to 200 people, as well as supplies for the journey, animals, and seeds to plant on their new island home.

Gilbert Islands

Solomon Islands

Tuvalu

Sturdy ships
Polynesian canoes were made from dug-out tree trunks with sails of palm-leaf matting and had outriggers to stabilize them; the ropes were made from coconut fibres.

Samoa Islands

smaller canoes used for fishing between local islands

Vanuatu

weaving baskets

Fiji Islands

Tonga

Cook Islands

Tahiti

New Caledonia
harvesting yams

catching coconuts from palm trees

South Pacific Ocean

Long-distance voyaging
Sea-going canoes had to sail at least 2,500km across open sea to reach Aotearoa.

The Maoris
The Polynesian settlers in Aotearoa became known as Maoris. Their warriors fought each other using sharp-edged clubs made of whalebone.

Woodcarving
Maoris carved statues of Pukaki, one of their main ancestors, out of wood.

AOTEAROA

hunting the moa (a flightless bird)

Dreamtime

Aboriginals believe that their ancestors were heroes who walked the earth during Tjukurpa, or Dreamtime. Some ancestors were human, others were animals and plants, or the sun, stars, wind and rain. They used certain paths, which link the land and the people together. Aboriginals retell the stories of Dreamtime from generation to generation, using paintings on rocks and walking along the sacred paths.

500BCE–1000CE

500BCE
500 Aboriginal peoples already well established in Australia and Solomon Islands

400BCE

300BCE
300 Polynesian culture develops in Fiji, Samoa and Tonga

200BCE
200 Polynesians sail east to Cook Islands and Tahiti

100BCE

0

100CE

200CE

300CE
300 Polynesians reach distant Easter Island in the eastern Pacific Ocean (not shown on map area)

400CE
400 Polynesians sail north from Marquesas to settle in the Line Islands and Hawaii (not shown on map area)

500CE

600CE

700CE

800CE

900CE
900s Polynesians sail south to settle in Aotearoa (New Zealand), where they are known as Maoris, and eventually the Chatham Islands

1000CE

Index

This index lists the main peoples, places and topics that you will find in the text in this book. It is not a full index of all the place names and physical features to be found on the maps.

Acknowledgements

The publisher would like to thank the following for permission to reproduce their material. Every care has been taken to trace copyright holders. However, if there have been unintentional omissions or failure to trace copyright holders, we apologize and will, if informed, endeavour to make corrections in any future edition.

Key: *b* = bottom, *c* = centre, *l* = left, *r* = right, *t* = top

Cover Aztec calendar The National Museum of Anthropology, Mexico City;
Parthenon with the kind permission of the Trustees of the British Museum, London;
6*tr* Alamy/Walter Bibikow/Jon Arnold Images; 6*b* Walter Bibikow/Photolibrary.com;
7*tl* Alamy; 7*tc* The Art Archive/Musée du Louvre, Paris/Dagli Orti; 7*tr* The Art Archive/
Archaeological Museum, Tikal, Guatemala/Dagli Orti; 7*bc* Corbis/Alfred Ko;
7*br* Corbis/SABA/Ricki Rosen; 9 Corbis/SABA/David Butow; 11 The Art Archive/British
Museum; 13 The Art Archive/Dagli Orti; 14*tr* Corbis/Sandro Vannini; 14*b* The Art Archive/
Musée du Louvre Paris/Dagli Orti; 15*t* The Art Archive/Musée du Louvre, Paris/Dagli Orti;
15*b* Corbis; 17 Corbis/Adam Woolfitt; 19 The Art Archive/National Museum, Karachi/Dagli Orti;
21 The Art Archive/Dagli Orti; 23 The Art Archive/Private Collection, Beirut/Dagli Orti;
25 Corbis; 27 Bridgeman British Museum; 28*tr* The Art Archive; 28*b* Corbis/Archivo
Iconografico, S.A.; 29*c* Getty/Giulio Andreini; 29*b* The Art Archive/Archaeological Museum,
Naples; 31 Corbis/Andrew Brown, Ecoscene; 32*tr* The Art Archive/Archaeological Museum,
Naples; 32*l* The Art Archive/Museo della Civilta Romana, Rome;
32–33*b* The Art Archive/Joseph Martin; 33*cl* Corbis/Reuters;
34 Werner Forman Archive; 37 *Sanchi* Alamy/Profimedia;
37 *Ramayana* The Art Archive/British Library; 38 The Art
Archive/Musée Guimet, Paris; 41 Corbis/Kevin Fleming;
43 *Chichén Itzá* Corbis/Michele Westmorland;
43 *Nazca pot* The Art Archive/Amano Museum,
Lima; 45 Corbis/Michael S. Yamashita.